The Spirit of
Youlgrave
& Alport

Bridget Ardley and Mary Bartlett

Published by

Landmark Publishing Ltd
Ashbourne Hall, Cokayne Ave, Ashbourne, Derbyshire DE6 1EJ England
Tel: (01335) 347349 Fax: (01335) 347303
e-mail: landmark@clara.net
web site: www.landmarkpublishing.co.uk

ISBN 1 84306 083 3

Print: Bath Press, Bath
Design: Mark Titterton
Cover: James Allsopp

Front cover: Fisherman's Cottage, Bradford Dale.
Page One: Holywell Lane.
Title page: All Saints' Church 100 years ago.
Back cover top: Cast of *Robinson Crusoe*, 1977.
Middle: Youlgrave All Saints' Tug of war team in training.
Bottom: A striking well dressing designed by Karen Sayer in 1998.

LANDMARK COLLECTOR'S LIBRARY

THE SPIRIT OF
YOULGRAVE
& ALPORT

THE 20TH CENTURY IN PHOTOGRAPHS

Bridget Ardley and Mary Bartlett

Landmark Publishing

Contents

At the beginning of the twenty first century Youlgrave and Alport are still real villages. Most of the inhabitants work locally, and some commute to Sheffield and further. Others, like the authors, are retired. Although some of the cottages have become holiday homes there is still a sense of community and the villages are in no way dormitories for the towns and cities. The links with the past are still strong. This may be explained by the continuity provided by a number of local families. There are now more houses, more cars, and more visitors. However, many names remain the same and people still attend church and chapel, enjoy well dressing and the band, and walk in the same beautiful dales.

These two school classes are divided by almost a century – a century of the fastest changes in human history. But they would surely recognise each other. In the first photograph are grandparents and great-grandparents of some of the children in the second.

There is a problem with the spelling of Youlgrave (or Youlgreave and many other versions) as there has been for centuries. The Rev. W Parker Stamper, in his booklet *A Derbyshire Village* (1902), chose the first spelling and so have we.

We hope that you will feel that this book represents the true spirit of the villages. The communities have evolved over the years and are held together by family ties and a sense of belonging. The past can be interpreted in different ways and people have not always agreed on the identification of various pictures. Please forgive us if we have got any names or dates wrong.

Acknowledgements

We were almost overwhelmed by the huge number of photographs that we were loaned and, inevitably, we have not been able to include them all. If we have not used your particular favourite, we apologise. We would like to thank the following for lending us photographs and other material, for giving us valuable information, trying to keep us on the right track and for encouraging us:

All Saints' School, Brian and Barbara Asquith, Bob Bache, Mildred Bacon, Peggy Bacon, Isobel Bailey, Chrissie Baker, Don Bateman, the Bell Ringers, Paul Blackmore, Alice Brassington, Colin and Shirley Brassington, Bill Brindley, David Camm, Lillian Clark, Pat Cleaver, Gordon Coupe, Edwina Edwards, Jennifer Elliott, Marie Evans, David Figg, Margaret Folley, Mary Froggatt, James and Cynthia Fryer, the George Hotel, Tom Gladwin, Granby House, Margaret Grant, Peter Hadfield, Frank and Muriel Harrison, Jeremy Hewitt, Margaret Holland, Peter Knowles, Sue Lomas, Bernard and Betty Oldfield, Dougie and Annette Oldfield, Ossie Post, Martha Prime, David and Ann Robinson, John Roper, Mick Roper, Cyril Rowland, Dorothy Sandell, Alastair Scrivener, Barbara Scrivener, Albert Shimwell, Chris and Irene Shimwell, Michael and Marjorie Shimwell, Sally Shimwell, Bob Skinner, Kath Smith, Malcolm Stacey, Leslie Toyne, the Village Hall, Mrs. Walker, Charlie and Eva Wardle, Ian Webster, Vince Webster, Minnie Wilson, Norman and Jan Wilson, Wendy Wilson, Mrs. Josie Wright, the YHA.

Drawings are reproduced with the kind permission of the artists Tricia Donnison (p.65) and Alastair Scrivener (p.8, 80).

Finally, we would like to dedicate this book to the memory of Bill Shimwell who, to many people, embodied the spirit of Youlgrave.

Alport in Winter.

All Saints' Church

For generations of local people this was a familiar scene, the village church approached along Church Street, with its splendid fifteenth century tower. With stonework dating from the twelfth century, almost certainly on an earlier site, it reflects the development of the community which it served for centuries. Many of the people who appear in this book were baptised, married, buried here.

The interior is a memorial to unnamed craftsmen who are part of the spirit of Youlgrave. Its Norman arches, mediaeval effigies and timber roof with strange carvings may well have been the work of ancestors of people living in the village now.

Above: This strange figure, tail between its legs, is high in the roof.

Above: The bat monster, also in the roof, appears rather differently in the village history play (p.146).

The effigy of Sir Thomas Cokayne, member of a local family and killed in a family brawl on his way back from church (not Youlgrave) in 1488, lies with his head on a cockerel, a reference to the family name.

Once music for services was provided by singers and stringed instruments, as the Churchwardens' Accounts tell us— '1796 Gave the singers towards a fiddle 0.10.6' and '1799 Gave to the singers for keeping the base good 0.7.6.'

Since 1862 there has been an organ as well as the choir and sometimes other instruments. The picture above shows Fred Billinge at the organ in the 1960s.

The choir in 1895 outside the vicarage in the time of the Rev. Stamper. Men and boys only at that date. Philip Rowland, Mildred Bacon's father, then aged ten, is on the right.

The choir after World War II, by that time augmented with female choristers.
In the second row from the back the two churchwardens, George Crisp on the left and Harry Holland flank the verger, Reginald Garratt. The schoolmaster Mr Lees sits to the right of the Rev. Hadfield. Also in the picture are H Wragg, N Brassington, H Moss, G Kenworthy, N Lever, J Rowland, Mrs Evans, Miss Oxley, S Boden, B Buxton, K Gladwin, B Evans, P Needham, A Robinson, B Moss, B Oldfield, P Dawson, J Boden, E Billinge, A Cawley.

The choir in full voice in Fountain Square for a well dressing service in the 1950s. Many familiar faces here, including Edith Rowland, Isobel Hadfield, Hilda Smedley, Isobel Bailey, Kathleen Tomlinson, Francesca Mayor and Mary Hall.

A church outing c.1958, with Ann and David Robinson, Mrs Stone, Mr Aspinall, Hilary Mills, Mrs Mills, Marjorie, Lucy and Harold Wardle.

Below are some vicars of All Saints'.

The Rev. Greenshields who retired in 1938. A bachelor living with his sister, he seems to have been very popular. Marie Evans remembers that the choir boys, including her future husband Frank, were given a generous 6d a week by the vicar.

The Rev. Hadfield outside the chancel door in the 1950s with churchwardens and vergers, G Crisp, H Holland, Mr Aspinall and R Garratt.

His successor Canon Roberts appears with bell ringers Jack Rowland and Nick Mercer (see p.17).

Above: The Rev. Derek Gibling who came as vicar of Youlgrave in 1977 was also a bee-keeper and a man of many talents. On the left he is shown on the chancel steps, with Ann Robinson and Margaret Pursglove. On the right he has abandoned his ecclesiastical garb for the costume of a gypsy chief with Mary Lomas as a gypsy maid in a memorable production of *The Sleeping Beauty* in 1978.

Above: The Rev. Ray Taylor preparing for a well dressing procession from the church, with Mrs Mills, David Robinson, Ann Hodgkinson and the Methodist minister, the Rev. Harby.

Right: The present incumbent, the Rev. Ossie Post.

There was a big Sunday School in the middle of the century, seen here with the Rev. and Mrs Hadfield and Mr and Mrs Lees in the centre, Louie Hadfield and Edith Rowland seated towards the right and many more that residents will recognise.

The church Sunday School in fancy dress c. 1955. It includes Joan Shimwell as Little Bo Peep, Irene Holland (now Shimwell) as Little Miss Muffet, Mary Holland as Mary, Mary Quite Contrary and Pat Birds and Lewis Twyford as Jack and Jill. In front is Harry Bourchier with a horn, and behind and to the right of Harry is John Wardle with what appears to be a duck.

The Girls' Friendly Society enjoying a holiday in Morecambe during World War 11, showing Kathleen Twyford, Mildred Rowland (now Bacon), Esme Holland, Dorothy Twyford, Freda Wragg, Lorna Taylor and Margaret Wragg.

Another GFS group in Bare, near Morecambe, with the Rev. and Mrs Hadfield, Kathleen Rowland, Barbara Titterton, Phyllis Holland,Ena Johnson, Sylvia Carter, Phyllis Hall, Brenda Shimwell, Stella Boden, Esme Holland and Cynthia Hall (now Fryer). Cynthia remembers that, since it was wartime, they had to take their own jam.

The church is decorated with flowers for sunday services and for special events. Here Mildred Bacon and Phyllis Needham decorate the pulpit for the wedding in December 1976 of Elizabeth Waterhouse and Richard Beckett, attended by the Prince of Wales and Princess Alexandra. New bell clappers were installed just in time for the event.

Below: Middleton Hall in 1982. The Duke of Devonshire crowns Sharon Lord Rose Queen, her twin sister Vetice in attendance. The girl guide behind is Emma Youatt.

Above: The church fete is an important annual event, here held in the vicarage garden in 1971.

The parish records have many references to payments to the bell ringers, ringing for national events. In 1711 the churchwardens recorded, 'To ye ringers upon ye news of ye victory over ye Spaniards. 0.2.6.' In those days they seemed to have consumed a quantity of ale; in 1800 Willm Pheasey was paid 0.10.0. 'for Ringers Ale'.

In 1870 William and Isabella Thornhill of Stanton-in-Peak gave a ring of eight bells in a bid to give Youlgrave the heaviest ring in the county, in which they succeeded until 1875 when St Luke's, Derby got ahead. They were cast by Mears and Stainbank, bell founders of London, to replace the previous five. The tenor, the heaviest bell at around 26 cwt., bears the inscription:

'I call the living, mourn the dead,
I tell when days and years are sped,
For grief and joy, for prayer and praise,
To heaven my tuneful voice I raise.'

Bell ringing, by its nature noisy, has not been universally popular, but on 16 July 1870, the Derbyshire Times recorded that 'the ringing of the new peal of bells was pronounced by competent judges to be very sweet, and at intervals during the day the whole neighbourhood resounded with the joyous clangour'.

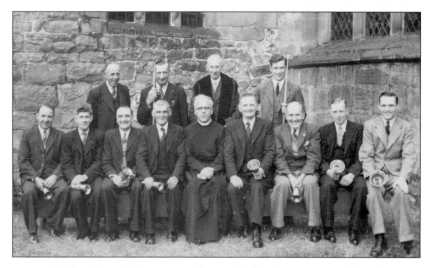

The ringers, vicar and churchwardens c.1950. At this time bell ringing was an exclusively male occupation. The ringers, gripping their hand bells, were more formally dressed than is considered obligatory nowadays.
In the picture are: B Allsop, G Crisp, R Garratt, H Holland, C Toft, E Billinge, L Ledger, H Toft(Leader), the Rev. Hadfield, N Brassington, J Rowland, H Slaney and H Moss.

Similarly, the traditional New Year's Eve supper in 1952 was men only. In the picture left, the then owner of the Old Hall, Mr Mayor, who dealt in wines and spirits, had provided the whisky, otherwise hard to obtain.

Standing at the back are: Bernard Allsop, George Crisp, Hugh Moss, Eric Billinge, Cliff Ledger, Norman Brassington; sitting facing are: Herbert Toft, the Rev. Hadfield, Nick Mercer, Mr Mayor, John Brindley, Arthur Boden, Harry Slaney; sitting in front, left to right: Reginald Garratt, Captain Wheatly-Crowe, Sidney Gilbert, Jack Rowland.

Above: The ringers in the early 1970s with three ladies: M Frost, E Rowland and K Roper.

Right: Ringing was often a family affair. Cyril Rowland rang for many years with his sister Edith and his cousin Jack, here being presented with a replica bell in 1974, on completing half a century of ringing.

He is flanked by Canon Roberts and Nick Mercer.

Some of the present band. Back row, from the left: Pat Cleaver, Eddie Oldfield, Alastair Scrivener, Ruth Littlewood, David Robinson, David Camm (Tower Captain); sitting: Leslie Toyne, Jackie Hodgkinson, Mary Bartlett, Laura Charlesworth and Ben Furness.

Bells and their frames do not last for ever and in 1937 the second bell cracked and funds had to be raised to recast it. The showing of Ronny Moore's village film was a contribution to that cost. Then after more than a century of use, ringing for services, baptisms, marriages, funerals, anniversaries and national events, all the bells had to be retuned and rehung in a new frame by Eayre and Smith of Melbourne and for a year between 1994 and 1995 the village was without bells. Above, the bells on their return from the foundry, outside the George Hotel.

The bells being transported across the road to the base of the tower and the difficult task of hauling them up into the belfry. One of them seems to have grown legs during its absence. Or is it David Camm in a new hat?

Much of the work of lowering the bells, removing more than a century's deposit of pigeon droppings and dead pigeons, then removing the old oak frame, was done by ringers and friends. In the pictures above and right David Robinson, then Tower Captain, is working among the wheels and thinking about the problem of getting many hundredweights of bell metal down a tower and up again.

Just when it seemed that the fund raising and heavy work were over, a new, lighter bell was donated to mark the golden jubilee of the Diocesan Association of Church Bell Ringers and money towards a second bell was raised, some given in memory of village people. It carries the inscription, 'I ring out in joyous remembrance of all the souls of Youlgreave'. The picture on the right shows the new bells being rung.

If you look up to the chancel roof you see a little turret where the ting tang bell hung. It is mentioned as early as 1760 when the churchwardens spent one shilling on 'a new rope for the ting tang'. Bill Shimwell and no doubt others remembered coming out of school at 10 o'clock on Pancake Tuesday to hear it rung.

Youlgrave was once well provided with chapels, built in the great days of flourishing non-conformity resulting from the preaching of John Wesley and others at the end of the eighteenth century.

In 1807 the first Wesleyan Chapel was built and a large Sunday School followed in 1887. The chapel was extended in 1907, an indication of its success.

The Primitive Methodists were a splinter group. Their first chapel at Bankside was built in 1822. In 1895 a new chapel and sunday school were built at Coldwell End. Marjorie Shimwell, in the Jubilee Souvenir Handbook published in 1945, explains that in 1895 the weather was so severe that there was no work in the quarries for seventeen weeks, so many quarrymen were available to prepare the ground for foundations, while the women and children cleared away the rubbish; truly a communal effort. On Good Friday the foundation stones were laid. Though the architect was Mr Harper of Nottingham, and many of the tenders recorded in the book were from Bakewell men, village craftsmen figure large, a mason called Shimwell and an Evans working in wood. Local names among the list of trustees include Birds, Brassington, Evans, Frost and Shimwell. The chapel is often referred to now as 'the top chapel'.

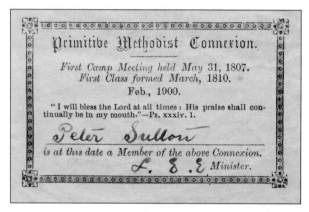

The admission of Peter Sutton to the Primitive Methodist Connexion in Feb. 1900.

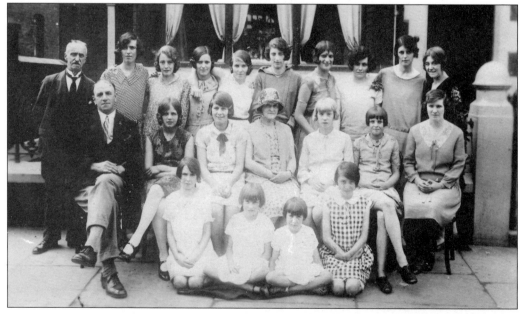

A Girls' Fellowship holiday in Blackpool c.1930. On the back row, from the left: John Dale, Elsie Hardy, Ena Nuttall, Minnie Webster, Gwen Bacon, Maud Nuttall, Alice Bacon, Josie Wright, Beryl Buxton; second row: ?, Mabel Holmes, Eleanor Bacon, Mrs Marsden, Alice Toft, Lilian Bacon, Mrs John Dale; Eileen, Cynthia and Joan Marsden and another little girl in front.

An event at the Primitive Methodist or Trinity Chapel in the 1930s. Back row, from the left: Mrs Dale, Mrs Lomas, Mrs Bacon, Mrs Hayes, Arthur Bacon, Mrs Mabel Shimwell, Frank Bacon; middle row: Mrs Oldfield, Mrs Hambleton, Mrs Jane Roper, Mrs Arthur Bacon, Jim Rowland, John Dale, Mr Lomas, Mrs Joe Birds, Mrs Wragg, Cynthia Marsden; front row: ?, Miss Gwen Bacon, Mrs Marjorie Shimwell, Mrs Mainprice, Mrs Ida Smith, Eileen Marsden, Joan Marsden, Freda Wragg. Mrs Mainprice, who lived at the Old Hall, has been presented with a bouquet. The two girls have not been identified.

Mrs Mainprice is remembered by Mrs Josie Wright as leading the group of WVS ladies who, during World War II, baked meat and potato pies on Tuesdays and Thursdays in the old Congregational Chapel. The WVS was allowed the ingredients, minced beef, potatoes, flour and fat. She also ran a 'children's clothing exchange' at the Old Hall during the period of clothing coupons.

A chapel trip to Chesterfield in 1937 by the famous Bacon choir, made up entirely of members of the Bacon family. On the back row, from the left (the surname is Bacon unless otherwise stated): Arthur, Jack Smith, Harold Jr, George Edwin, Joseph Hayes, Alan, Harold Snr, Frank; middle row: Eleanor (later Mrs Rose of the newsagents), Sarah Ann Hayes (née Bacon), Gertrude, Maud, Mabel, Emily; front row: Gilbert, Gwen, Cynthia Marsden, Ida Smith (née Bacon), Mrs Bacon, Joan Marsden, Eileen Marsden, Lilian. Twice before World War II the Bacon choir broadcast from Leeds.

Above: A nativity play in the 1930s.

Trinity Methodist Church, Youlgrave

1895

Jubilee Souvenir Handbook

1945

Left: The Jubilee Souvenir Handbook produced in 1945 by Marjorie Shimwell. The Jubilee celebrations started on 14 July with a bazaar and sale of work opened by the local benefactress Miss Melland.

Below: Maypole dancing c.1939.

Further divisions led to the building of the Wesleyan Reform Chapel in 1857 on land provided by W P Thornhill of Stanton Hall. In 1860 a schoolroom was added and the building extended in 1886 and 1913.

It was provided with electric lighting by E J Evans and Co.

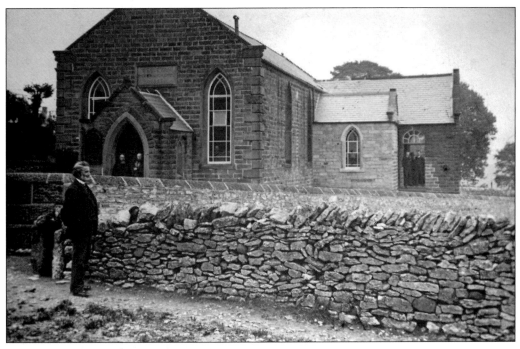

The picture above, pre-1900, shows the chapel before the road surface down Holywell Lane was properly made up. Where Brookleton and Pretoria now are there was a field, accessible through a stile by the chapel wall.

Members of the congregation pictured outside before 1900. Standing, from the left: David Thompson, James Evans, Mrs John Evans, Edwin James Evans; seated: Mrs John Toft, John Toft, Mrs James Evans. Mr and Mrs James Evans were Alice Brassington's great grandparents, Edwin James Evans her grandfather.

Left: The 1957 centenary celebrations, showing Evelyn Wood, Mrs Walker, Avril Fryer, Mrs F G Nuttall, the Rev. Finnemore, Arnold Prince, Herbert Evans, Leslie Wild, Gregory Hadfield.

In the 1950s the Sunday School enjoyed outings to Trentham Gardens and to Maplethorpe. Going to Trentham Gardens, right, were Mr and Mrs Elsey, Christine Camm (née Walker), Mr and Mrs Lincoln, Mr and Mrs G Hadfield, Susan and Janice Lincoln and Sally Shimwell (née Hadfield) with Robert and John.

Below: Among those enjoying Maplethorpe in 1958 were T Hadfield, I Wright, D Needham, R Walker. Teenagers nowadays would not be so smartly dressed for the seaside.

The Congregational Chapel was built for Thomas Bateman of Lomberdale, the nineteenth-century antiquary and arch enemy of the vicar of Youlgrave. He had vowed never to enter Youlgrave church again, and he did not, being buried in a field at Middleton. The chapel was built in Bateman's interpretation of the romanesque style, simple and with round arches. It did not flourish as the other chapels were doing and was turned to other uses.

In 1927 it became a domestic science centre for the school and during World War II was used by the WVS. People could take their fruit and sugar and have it made into jam. In 1955 it became the headquarters of the Youlgrave branch of the Royal British Legion.

Of these architectural reminders of the strength of nineteenth- and twentieth-century nonconformity only two still thrive and perform their original purpose; the others converted to other uses.

Youlgrave School as it is now with the children's section of the churchyard in front.

There was once a small school on the site of the present YHA building, but the present village school dates from 1868. It was built on land donated by the Duke of Rutland, in gritstone and limestone, probably by William Shimwell, 'Old Will'. The building was divided into two rooms by a wooden screen, folding back on wrought-iron hinges stamped with the name of the village blacksmith, Eli Toft, and the date 1869. Bill Shimwell said that when he was teaching there he kept the stamp visible through a series of repaintings. 'Old Will' also built the Primitive Methodist Chapel in 1895 and carved the bull on the Bull's Head. The infants' department was added in 1892. In 1980 a dining/assembly hall and a kitchen were completed and inside toilets in 1996. Prior to the building of the dining room the children were taken in a crocodile to eat their lunches in the upstairs room of the George.

A happy picture from the 1920s with; Back row, from left: Reg Evans, Wesley Bateman, Dick Thompson, Harold Wardle, Edwin Billinge, Frank Evans, Bob Rowland, ? Oldfield 3rd row: Olive Grasham, Carrie Shimwell, Maud Thornhill, Mary Holland, Connie Shimwell, Freda Stevenson, Marion Shimwell, Mary Finney, Ada Toft, Mabel Holmes, Betty Rowland 2nd row: Grace Taylor, Kathleen Harrison, Eleanor Bacon, Doris Birds, Alice Marshall, Sadie Bateman, Louie Birds, Alice Rowland, Lilian Bacon Front row: Lionel Carter, Sid Brassington, Harry Birds, Cedric Hill, Leonard Penny, Jim Frost, Lawrence Shimwell, Donald Walker, Philip Rowland
School master - Mr Gimber.

At school in 1921. It is thought that the very young children, the girl 3rd from the left and the boy 2nd from the right in the front row, were not yet pupils but had come along for the photograph. The little boy in his sailor hat was Mildred Bacon's brother Philip, then about four. The little girl, unnamed, is wearing her best shoes, while the others wear boots.

These are older pupils in 1925 with Miss Libby Rowland, assistant teacher.

A cookery class c.1927, probably at the ex-Congregational Chapel which was used by the school. It shows Eleanor Bacon, Ada Toft, Mary Finney, Connie Shimwell, Mary Walker, Betty Rowland, Olive Gresham, Dorothy Birds, Marion Shimwell, Freda Stevenson, Carrie Shimwell, Mabel Holmes, Maud Thornhill, Louie Birds, Lilian Bacon and Alice Marshall.

Eleanor Smith (1862-1942; née Thompson), a formidable-looking lady, was not Youlgrave by birth but certainly by adoption. She taught in the school in the early twentieth century and became head of the infants' department. Her grand-daughter, Muriel Harrison, appropriately now living in the School House, remembers being taken to school by 'Granny Smith' on her first day. Muriel's mother was so upset at 'losing' her last child that she could not take her. Mrs Smith was a pillar of the church and took the young Muriel three times every Sunday.

A surprising number of photographs have survived from the 1920s, clearly much treasured. Seated in the school yard with their teacher Martha Pursglove, Bill Shimwell identified George Oldfield, Eric Hollis, ? Fraser, Teddy Twyford, Leonard Taylor, Bill Slaney, Enos Wragg, Tom Holmes, himself, Nancy Webster, Mary Brindley, Julia Briddon, Marion Shimwell, Jim Frost, Carrie Shimwell, Eleanor Bacon, Nellie Evans and Maud Thornhill. Bill had been told to keep his chin up and he did.

The children in the very early photographs often look overawed, either by the camera or the teacher, but this pre-World War II group looks much more relaxed. On the back row are, from the left: Hedley Toft, Ronald Birds, Avis Wragg, Nora Yates, Sylvia Frost, Joyce Evans, Hilda Elliott, Kathleen Scriven, Kenneth Gratton, Ben Rowland and ?. On the front row are: Doris Marshall, Cyril Warren, Luther Shimwell, Frank Twyford, Clifford Hayward, Maurice Gladwin and Joyce Birds.

Some people are amazing at remembering how they and their friends looked half a century ago.

In this infants' class group photo of about 1947 most have been identified. Perhaps some readers will be able to fill the gaps.

Standing at the back, from the left: Mrs Owen, head of the infants' school, Phyllis Hall, a student teacher, and Mrs Lees, reception teacher; on the back row: Hilary Birds, Alice ?, Ruth Wild, Angela Frost, Christine Shimwell, Olive Marsden, Merle Cawley, Dorothy Gilbert, Maureen Wragg, Annette Bosley, Wendy Bosley, Joan Smedley, Elizabeth ?; on the middle row: Tom Hadfield, Ian Colman, Robert Walker, Tommie Marsden, David Brassington, David Needham, ?, ?, Colin Brassington, Vic Prime, David Birds, Thomas Elliott, Malcolm Webster; on the front row: Sam Billinge, Peter Wragg, Helen Kilbride, ? Smedley, Jean ?, Pearl Webster, Hilda Smedley, Margaret Roper, ?, Pat Mellor, Shirley Wagstaffe, Raymond ?, Ian Wright.

The infants in 1967 with Mrs Thompson and the head mistress, Mrs Gregory.

From the back, left to right: Ian Harland, Stephen Oldfield, Desmond Rhodes, David Cardwell, Martin Harrison, Nicholas Cordin, Stephen Ring, Tony Stacey, Trevor Hollis; Simon Frost, Robert Phillips, Lynn Birds, Susan Green, Deborah Bourne, Jane Brindley, Margaret Charlesworth, Wendy Birds, Sally Anne Grant, Valerie Rhodes, Jeremy Bacon, Bernard Charlesworth; Jane Beattie, Julie Upton, Linda Bacon, Donna Oldfield, Ann and Alison Carter, Susan Holland, Janice Wilson, Sharon Bottom; Nigel Evans, Ian Roper, Jeffrey Wilson, Nicholas Harcus, Jenny Young, Susan Carson, Mandy Oldfield, Paul Riley, Gordon Bacon, Robert Fell.

At this date the infant and junior schools were separate, though in the same building. The yard was divided by a wall.

Youlgrave won the Bunting Cup for the second time in 1969, wearing the same shirts as in 1952. Back row, from the left: Robin Stacey, Peter Elliott, Trevor Sellors, Barry Oldfield, Philip Wragg, Mark Swindell, Jeremy Hall; front row: Chris Stone, Richard Bacon, David Bosley, Kevin Jackson, David Shimwell.

School group in 1977, with Mr Shimwell, Mrs Holland, the headmaster Mr Fraser.
On the back row, left to right: Martin Hill, Leslie Birds, Anthony Young, Robert Evans, Douglas Oldfield, Andrew Thorpe, David Nuttall; 4th row: David Carslaw, Mark Wain, John Carter, Alan Brownlee, Julian Sanderson, Andrew Bidmead, Keith Harrop, Peter Hill, Paul Carnell, Julian Wheeldon, Richard Foxley, Peter Ashmore, Paul Griffin, Alan Falder; 3rd row: Ruth Baker, Denise Parker, Jane Andrews, Mandy Gill, Julia Wardle, Lesley Brassington , Ruth Bristow, Susan Parker, Emma Barton, Jayne Bristow, Tracy Roper, Katharine Holland, Deborah Gilbert, Susan Hawkins; 2nd row: Sandra Harrop, Lisa Oldfield, Claire Bristow, Susannah Hall, Jeanette Shimwell, Sharon McNevin, Susanne Foxley, Jacqueline Parker, Jane Birds, Frances Nuttall, Susan Brassington, Genevieve Wilson, Emma Youatt; Front row: Steven Evans, Kevan Parker, Jonathan Hall, David Gibson, Adrian Wheeldon, Michael Hadfield, Mark Oldfield, Barry Ollerenshaw, Philip McCaul, Michael Youatt, Alan Bacon, John Carter, Martin Parker.

A school group from early in the twentieth century and the school millennium photograph are in the introduction. The adults on the latter are Andrea Harrison, Helen Wragg, Heather Wood, Paul Hayes, Shaun Snow, Pam Stacey, Susan Barradell, Hilary Hawley and Kathy Wildgoose.

The school staff in the Jubilee year of 1977. Standing from left to right: Bill Shimwell, deputy head of the junior school, Mrs F Lomas, welfare assistant in the infants school, Mrs S Thompson, reception class teacher, Mrs A Gregory, head of the infants school, Mrs C Baker, part-time teacher in the junior school, Mrs M Holland, teacher of 1st and 2nd years in the junior school, Mr J Fraser, head of the junior school; sitting are: Mrs A Robinson, secretary and Mrs M Skinner, welfare assistant in the junior school.

There have always been special events throughout the school year.

A nativity play in the early 1960s, with Janice Lincoln as Mary, Helen Bacon, Patricia Smith and Linda Andrews as the three kings, but who is Joseph?

A school play in church in the late 60s. Wendy Wilson remembers it as to do with Noah's Ark, since Sally Ann Grant was a dove. At first we thought that there were fairies and we wondered what fairies were doing in the ark. However Mrs Lomas remembers doing the costumes and thinks that the children shown are raindrops. Wendy is in the front row, right, with the Carter twins behind her. Also identified are Susan Green, Margaret Charlesworth and Jane Brindley.

The playgroup showing off their Easter bonnets, c.1974. Nicola Bacon, Amy Tabbenor, Kevin Allsop, Cathy Shimwell, Richard Partridge, Caroline Atkin and Nicola Shimwell are among them.

In 1971 the school produced a pageant in church to help the roof restoration fund. It enacted some of the events from village history. In this picture, remembering the year 950 AD, news has reached Giolgrave (another spelling of Youlgrave) that a travelling priest has arrived at the hall and will soon be at the village cross to heal the sick and give his blessings. The lady of the manor will give alms to the poor. The priest is played by Peter Wilson and the lady by Kate Connolly. Other performers were Jane Beattie, Lynn Birds, Wendy Birds, Susan Carson, Margaret Charlesworth, Donna Oldfield and Susan Green.

This scene refers to the Jacobite Rebellion of 1745 and an entry in the church records states that the churchwardens 'paid to George Toft the village constable the sum of 6 pence' to move on the retreating highlanders who were roaming the countryside. Among those taking part were Graham Dawson, Nigel Hollis, Jeremy Bacon, Richard Birds and Ian Roper.

Mr Lees' retiring party in 1963, showing, from the left: Mrs Lees, Mr Lees, the Rev. Hadfield, Helen Bacon. He has been presented with a gramophone.

The staff and a visitor in the late 1970s. Back row, left to right: Ann Robinson, Eileen Bacon, Peggy Skinner, Violet Bacon, Dorothy Sandell; front row: Mary Lomas, Bill Shimwell, Ann Gregory, ?, John Fraser, Shirley Thompson, Margaret Holland.

Ann Gregory's leaving party in 1978. We leave you to recognise yourself or your child.

Bill Shimwell retired in 1979 after 31 years in the school. Also in the picture are Tom Gladwin, Marion Frost and Gwyneth Brindley and many other members of his first class of 1948.

Since 1992 Youlgrave has been linked with the village of Bangbutt in Sierra Leone through the charity Village Aid. Schoolchildren exchange letters with children in Bangbutt and fund-raising in Youlgrave is helping the people of Bangbutt to rebuild their village after the devastating civil war.

The school bell was first hung in 1868, the date stamped on the bell, contemporary with the building of the school. However, the turret was considered unsafe and the bell taken down before or during the last war and 'sat under a desk in the office for many years'.

It was restored by craftsmen at Middleton-by-Wirksworth Mine and rung again on 13 December 2001. It calls the children to school at 8.50 each morning, though according to Mr Snow, not hearing it is no excuse to stay away.

The picture above shows Jeremy Hewitt, Oliver Harrop, Joe Wilkin, Adam Wilson, Sam Brassington, Ryan Tabbenor, Gemma Dawson and the soon-to-retire headmaster, Mr Snow.

In 1955 the old Congregational Chapel was purchased by the Youlgreave Branch of the Royal British Legion as their centre and social club, being named The Knoll Club after a neighbouring hillock.

The Royal British Legion parade past the Bull's Head for the dedication of a new standard in 1981. On the left, the World War I veterans, V Wilson, B Gladwin, T Brassington; on the dais the Lord Lieutenant Col. Peter Hilton, the High Sheriff Major Hugo Waterhouse; behind are Major General Peter Cavendish and Captain Beeley; to the right J Boden, Chairman of the Parish Council, the Chairman of Derbyshire Dales District Council and N Wilson , all flanked by the standard bearers.

A British Legion dinner at the Bull's Head in the 1950s. Among the guests are Mrs Cavendish, Alethea Birds, Lilian Brassington, Ted Craw, Minnie Wagstaffe and Harold Wragg.

The standards carried from Grove Place towards the church for a Remembrance Day service.

Only the British Legion still has a parade but in the past Friendly Societies had midsummer parades and feasts. These societies, in pre-welfare state days, helped their members, financially and otherwise, in times of hardship. Once the village had Foresters, Druids, Oddfellows and the Rechabites for the teetotallers. The Royal Antediluvian Order of Buffaloes, the 'Buffs', still survives in the village. Society banners are still stored in the church.

Here the Ancient Order of Foresters, in appropriate costume, parade the banner of the order towards the church, with a band behind, in the 1930s. It shows Arthur Marsden, High Chief Ranger of the order. He built Turret House. To the right is the old monumental mason's workshop and to the left the corner of the Thornhill Arms. Marie Evans remembers that when Arthur Marsden was made High Chief Ranger his car, with himself inside, was pulled in triumph through the village.

Before 1914 the members of 'the Buffs' used to meet in the George Hotel and the landlady, Mrs Briggs, can be seen here, third from the right on the second row. The two men seated on the left of the front row are Frank Evans and Arthur Wardle. Later Frank's son, Frank, and Arthur's daughter, Marie, would marry, though the two men could not have known this at the time. In the middle of the front row is Mr Throp, the schoolmaster.

The document recording the election of Brother Arthur Wardle as Knight of the Order of Merit on 30 September 1925. Charlie Wardle still has his father's regalia.

The Buffs in the 1930s included George Bacon, Billy Stone, Eric Billinge, Billy Boden, Harry Ollerenshaw (blacksmith and waterworks manager), Ernest Shimwell, Dan Prime, Enos Wragg, Jim Rowland (flag bearer), Joseph Evans, Jack Fearn, Abraham Evans, Billy Hill, Tom Cassel, Joe Walker, Harry Oldfield, Harold Colman (Miss Melland's chauffeur).

In 1964 the Buffs held their feast in celebration of sixty years of the Lathkill Lodge. Left to right standing are: A Shimwell, H Wheeldon, G Crisp, A Oldfield, A Prime, P Noton, T Cassels, G Roper, H Moss; sitting are: E Billinge, T Housley, H Desforges, the Grand Primo, J Rowland, B Hambleton, C Frost and H Shimwell.

Many local men died during the two World Wars as can be seen on the Rolls of Honour in the church. Others survived. Some were in the Home Guard and others served in peacetime. Youlgrave did not escape bomb damage during World War II. We are told that a 1000 lb. bomb hit Conksbury Farm taking off the roof and doors. The explosion was such that pieces of kale from a nearby field were found in Over Haddon and part of the bomb casing in Alport. Incendiary bombs caused considerable damage from the Bull's Head to Coldwell End. Fires caused by these were put out either by villagers or by "Youlgrave Fire Brigade" – a trailer pump on the back of a car. One such device apparently slid down the ramp towards the basement of the Co-op (now the YHA) and was kicked away by a guest at the Bull's Head. On another occasion a returning British bomber crashed into the river Lathkill above Conksbury Bridge, its crew having parachuted to safety landing in Chatsworth Park.

Harry Holland Sr.'s Certificate of Service dated 1908.

Luther Shimwell (seated) with a friend in Belgium during World War I.

Men of the Derbyshire Yeomanry during World War I. Harry Holland Sr. is standing on the left.

Youlgrave men serving during World War I. On the l. in the back row is Eddie Evans and Colin Gregory is on the r. In the middle, seated, is Herbert Evans and Louis Throp is on the r. He was gassed and died in 1924 aged 30.

A postcard sent home during World War I. Harry Holland Sr. is second from l. He wrote: "They look a funny lot, don't they?"

Dorothy Harrison joined the ATS during World War II.

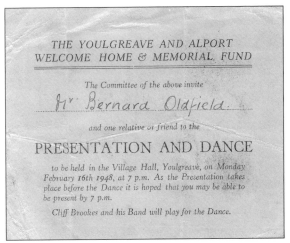

THE YOULGREAVE AND ALPORT
WELCOME HOME & MEMORIAL FUND

The Committee of the above invite

Mr Bernard Oldfield

and one relative or friend to the

PRESENTATION AND DANCE

to be held in the Village Hall, Youlgreave, on Monday February 16th 1948, at 7 p.m. As the Presentation takes place before the Dance it is hoped that you may be able to be present by 7 p.m.

Cliff Brookes and his Band will play for the Dance.

In February 1948 180 men and women from Youlgrave, Harthill and Alport who served in World War II were welcomed home at an event organised by the Welcome Home and War Memorial Committee. Mr A E Harrison is shown presenting a gift to Mr D Birds. Mr R Wagstaffe is on the right. Bernard Oldfield's invitation to the event is shown above.

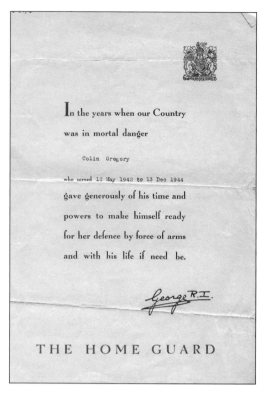

This scroll commemorates

Fusilier H. Birds
Royal Inniskilling Fusiliers

held in honour as one who
served King and Country in
the world war of 1939-1945
and gave his life to save
mankind from tyranny. May
his sacrifice help to bring
the peace and freedom for
which he died.

In the years when our Country
was in mortal danger

Colin Gregory

who served 12 May 1942 to 13 Dec 1944

gave generously of his time and
powers to make himself ready
for her defence by force of arms
and with his life if need be.

George R.I.

THE HOME GUARD

Martha Prime's brother, Fusilier H Birds, was killed
in World War II. She has this Commemorative Scroll
hanging in her sitting room.

A Home Guard Certificate.

Peggy Bacon was in the WAAF in 1942. She is in the back row, 2ⁿᵈ from r., in this WAAF hockey team.

Colin Gregory's Certificate of Proficiency for the Home Guard, dated 1944.

Charlie Wardle was in the Home Guard during World War II.

In the early 1970s Mary Turner (née Holland) taking part in her Passing Out parade in the WRNS.

The craft of Well Dressing has a particular significance in Youlgrave. It is thought to have started in 1829 to celebrate the arrival of a piped water supply from springs outside the village. The village still has a private water supply though not entirely from the original springs (see the chapter on Youlgrave Waterworks). In 1829 the Fountain, a circular cistern in the centre of the village, was erected and the supply was piped to it (see p.62). The Fountain was decorated in celebration and the custom continued for about 20 years. Well dressing was revived in 1869 when several taps were installed at various points in the village. It has continued, with few breaks, since then. It can be argued that our custom should be called 'Tap Dressing', but the more traditional name prevails. Youlgrave dresses five 'wells' in June and the craft has reached a particularly high standard. Many people travel from different parts of the country to admire the designs and marvel at the skill of the welldressers.

Although the subject of well dressing designs in Youlgrave is frequently biblical or at least illustrates a biblical text this is not always so. In 1928, when all five dressings were designed by Mr George Gimber the schoolteacher, the Fountain Well celebrated the British Empire with a depiction of the Taj Mahal in India.

A welldresser at work.

Getting the boards out of the river Bradford where they have soaked for 10 days. Visitors, seeing the boards in the water, have been heard to comment on the vandals who throw rubbish into the river. Simon Frost is on the trailer as John Roper and Ron Shimwell lift the board. They are watched by Colin Brassington and a young boy.

Frank Wilson and Jim Shimwell are seen in Old Hall Farm yard engaged in putting the puddled clay on to the boards.

Fred Billinge is seen (right) helping at a well dressing.

More well dressers at work.

In 1987, a visitor watches the complicated procedure of erecting the Fountain Well dressing in the early hours of Saturday morning. John Groom is tying the ropes on the left.

The procession coming back along Church Street following the Blessing of the Wells in 1962. The church choir and the band can be seen.

In the 1960s the well dressers enjoyed a dinner at the George Hotel. Among those present were Jeff Webster, Sally Hadfield, Shirley Wagstaffe, Minnie and Margaret Webster, Colin Brassington, Les Dyson, Norman Wilson, Dorothy Gilbert, John Bacon, Kath Gilbert, Derek Oldfield, Joyce Oldfield, Fred Shimwell, Eric Billinge and Freda Lomas.

Some of the 1977 well dressers outside the Village Hall. From l to r: Chrissie Baker (née Shimwell), Sheila Harding, Jim Evans, Margaret Fell (née Boardman), Ivy Evans, Bill Baker, Norman Wilson, Fred Shimwell, Malcolm Nix, Ruth McGrath (née Mercer), Dorothy Shimwell, Jim Shimwell, Emily Chapman, Frank Wilson.

The Fountain Well. In the background can be seen the name of Shimwell's shop (now the Post Office).

Left: In 1979 Youlgrave Waterworks celebrated its 150th anniversary and the distinguished artist John Piper was invited to design the Fountain Well to mark the occasion. He is seen here in the shed. Chrissie Baker (née Shimwell) is on the right.

Below: Malcolm Nix discusses the well dressing with John and Myfanwy Piper in 1979.

When John Piper designed the Fountain Well he wasn't told to include the text so it had to be put on a separate board. The children are (l to r): Cassie Worth, Jane Ardley, Liam Worth and Lenka Worth.

John Piper's design caused some controversy as it was unlike more conventional well dressings. But the Fountain Well has long had a reputation for being different....

A well dressing in 1926 when it was the custom to add garlands.

1905, with garlands.

The Coldwell End well dressing when it stood at the original tap spot.

This may have been during the Jubilee celebrations in 1935. It was obviously a special occasion, probably royal, as the Fountain has been dressed on two or three sides instead of the usual one, a Union flag is flying and there is a crown on the headboard. Note also Shimwell's shop (the present Post Office) and the farm buildings to the left. It looks as if someone was living in Thimble Hall.

In the 1920s the Duke and Duchess of Rutland brought Lady Diana Duff Cooper (née Manners) and other guests to see the well dressing that portrayed his home at Belvoir Castle.

An early dressing at the Reading Room. We are told that Marie Evans (née Wardle) and Dorothy Sandell (née Wardle) may be among the little girls.

An early aerial view of the church, Church Street, Conksbury Lane and the top of Bradford Lane.

Youlgrave and Alport have houses from the modest to the grand, from the seventeenth century to the twentieth, reflecting the different ways of life within the village community.

One of the earliest buildings is Monks' Hall or Old Hall in Alport, close to the junction of the rivers Bradford and Lathkill.

Monks' Hall is said to have been the home of Sir Roger Rooe and family who are commemorated on an early seventeenth century memorial in the church. Three centuries later Ben and Cyril Rowland stand by the gate of the right hand house where they were born. Later the family moved to the left hand part of the building where Cyril spent most of his life, with his sister Edith who contributed so much to village life and appears in some of the choir pictures and among the bell ringers.

In Youlgrave the original Old Hall, now Old Hall Farm, dates from c.1630. An early photograph calls it the Old Manor Farm. For much of its history it was a working farm, in the days when farms were within the village rather than on the outskirts, a splendid building with a yard that would once have been bursting with agricultural activity and timber haulage. It was sold to the Shimwell family in 1921 by the Duke of Rutland and remained in their hands for most of the century. It is now a private house.

The Old Hall, also dating from the seventeenth century but with later additions, was never intended to be on a busy road with cars parked in front but it looks at home in this picture from the early twentieth century with a pinafored girl with a pram, boys with a hoop and gentle traffic.

The Old Hall stables were conveniently across the quiet road, but this is the road now. Youlgrave is a working village so lorries pass through, and a holiday area also. Though there are car parks at the edge of the village, Youlgrave has spectacular traffic jams.

When the Old Stables in Main Street really was a stables at the beginning of the twentieth century it was the 'horseman's daily duty' to drive the owner of the Old Hall to Rowsley station in a pony and trap.

The handsome eighteenth-century houses on the north side of Church Street suggest affluence and comfort. Lathkill House was also a bank until about twenty years ago, the customers waiting in the hall. Auburn House, built in 1734, was the home of members of the Coates family, makers of sewing cotton. Later St Vincent's in Conksbury Lane was built for the Wills' tobacco family. Rich families were appreciating the pleasures of life in Youlgrave.

The naming of houses is often interesting. Pretoria, at the top of Holywell Lane, home of the Evans and Brassington families since its completion, was built by E J Evans, joiner and undertaker, in 1900. It was named to celebrate the capture of Pretoria in the Boer War.

Wembley House at Coldwell End was built in 1925 for John Birds and named to celebrate his successful expedition to Wembley to see the British Empire Exhibition.

Sheldon House on the left of the picture was named after an influential local family, remembered in the church and churchyard and registered as gentry in nineteenth-century directories.

Raenstor Close was built in 1911 by Frederick Gladstone Nuttall (a splendid name) for the Misses Melland. He attempted to make it look older than it is, by devices like blocked up windows. The picture above (l) shows builders on the site, that on the right Miss Melland, who gave the playing fields and village hall to the community.

To each side of the main gate are relief carvings of the animals charmed by Orpheus. They are the work of a local craftsman, Charles Webster.

Whytecote in Church Street, on the site of an earlier farm, was built c. 1907. In its day it was experimental, in the style of the architect C F A Voysey, influenced by the Arts and Crafts Movement and by Charles Rennie Mackintosh. Written on the back of the postcard reproduced below are the words 'Went to work in this house early in 1914 at Dr Byrne's, 2/6 a week'. For a time this was one of the many homes of the Youlgrave surgery. On the left is Mrs Staley in the formal front garden.

By comparison with the cottages, the fine seventeenth and eighteenth-century houses and the solid nineteenth and twentieth-century family houses, Raenstor Close and Whytecote are untypical, as is Hopton Turret House, built in the last decade of the twentieth century by a local architect Robert Bacon. Yet they all blend in with the originality of their designs and the quality of their stonework and contribute to the satisfying variety of village buildings.

Some buildings, familiar a century ago, have disappeared, surviving only in a levelling of the ground and in photographs. The Fisherman's Cottage on the south side of the Bradford at the bottom of Holywell Lane looks idyllic but it must have been damp and dark in winter.

This picture was taken on the day before it was demolished in the early 1950s. Eva Wardle is on the right.

The last thatched cottages, above the Knoll Club, disappeared in the 1920s, but Thimble Hall remains, right of the Fountain in the above picture. The tiny white cottage in Fountain Square became news recently when it was on the property market, though no-one suggested that it would make a family home again. To the left was Dunn's shop, selling sweets and tobacco, now the post office.

A view of the Boarding House Hotel on Alport Hill, once a private residence, then a hotel, demolished just before World War II to straighten the road and make it safer. Pictures in the section on transport show just how necessary that was. On the right of the picture is Lathkill House Farm. Here too was the area of the cockpit, which no doubt provided excitement for some but, according to the Rev. Stamper, writing in 1902, aroused the indignation of an earlier vicar, a man 'of commanding presence', who would disperse the participants and walk away with the cockerels.

Early in the century Lathkill House Farm had a tea garden and a construction of tufa in the garden. The pitted volcanic rock outcrops only a hundred yards away. The tea garden was where the arches are but they were later demolished and used to make a rockery. The Mosleys farmed there from the 1930s until the 1990s. Now it is a private house.

Isobel Mosley (now Bailey) moved to Brook View, once a lead miner's cottage, with separate entrance for the horse, now blocked up on the left.

Alport before Bridge House was built. Once there was a pub on the site.

The Gables stands at the end of the site of Knocking Alley, famous to people who have lived all their lives in the village. For people new to the village, Knocking Alley was a row of cottages at right angles to Coldwell End above Bradford Dale and so called because there the lead ore was separated from the rock, largely by the women, on a floor of rock or pavers. Originally owned by individuals, the cottages became the property of George Fowler, manager of the Co-op, and became known as Fowler's Row, but Knocking Alley is a more interesting name.

Large families were brought up in Knocking Alley. This shows the Oldfield family. Edith, in the middle of the back row, married Clement Shimwell and brought up her brother's child Dougie, along with her own large family. Dougie Oldfield's grandparents are in the middle of the front row.

On the left is a much worn but historic photograph of the demolition of Knocking Alley; on the right an imaginative reconstruction of Knocking Alley from verbal descriptions. Sanitation cannot have been up to modern standards in the crowded cottages on Bankside a century ago. One of the authors, when a member of the Parish Council and relatively new to the village, was for a long time confused by a past chairman and his frequent references to Shitty Lane.

By the 1930s houses were being built down Bradford Lane. These two photographs show, on the left, the foundations for the houses now often referred to as Mount Pleasant, and, below, the bottom of Bradford before the cottages were built facing the river. Below Mount Pleasant there was once a barn and smithy where Owl Cottage now stands.

After World War II new houses were needed and were built at Grove Place on the site of the Old Close and at Mawstone. The picture on the left shows the first phase of building at Old Close, and below, a recognisable Grove Place.

Looking down to Mawstone.

At the end of the century, starter homes were built towards the bottom of Bradford. The older cottages are to the left and the church tower behind.

Many buildings have changed their use over the years. Shops have turned into houses and the Co-op into the Youth Hostel. Granby House has seen many changes. Built in the early 1900s as a guest house, it became a doctor's house and surgery, then a knitwear factory, now it is an Abbeyfield Home.

Left: Granby House with its original owners. Martha Birds is in the centre.

Five doctors in a row worked from Granby House, starting with Dr Steele, ending with Dr Ivers, after which the doctors had a portacabin at the top of Bradford, until they moved into the new surgery opposite Granby House in 1995. Some people remember the first doctors setting out in a pony trap; now they leave by car.

The conversion of Granby House to an Abbeyfield Home and its subsequent running was and is the work of a dedicated band of volunteers.

It was opened in 1990 by the Prince and Princess of Wales who are shown on the left with Joy Stubbs, Pat Cleaver and David Figg, and on the right with Lady Caroline Waterhouse.

Below left, the Prince of Wales with Dorothy Harrison, Mildred Bacon, Marie Evans and the Lord Lieutenant Peter Hilton. Right and below, a royal walkabout, the Prince and Princess of Wales meeting the village.

The Village Hall is central to village life. It was given by Mrs T C Waterhouse of Lomberdale Hall and the Misses Melland of Raenstor Close in 1909. At that time the temperance movement was strong and the demon drink was not allowed inside. The Band of Hope met there and the YMCA. The secretary Mr Percy Smith was an ex-missionary and formed a football team to play against the village team. They met at Shogdale but the temperance team was unimpressive and scorned as 'the pussyfoots'. At the beginning of the century there were thatched cottages where the hall now stands. In the photograph on the left, taken in the 1970s, it does not look its best since new toilets were being built. It shows one of the two modern versions of the village's name. It also appears in the section on well dressing (p.50).

Shops, pubs and a post office are the lifeline of a community. Let them go and a cluster of houses, however agreeable, does not make a village. In 2003 Youlgrave still has these necessities, three pubs, three shops, a post office and a teashop. However, look back not too far and there was a community with more shops and pubs, when people did not go so regularly to Bakewell, Matlock, Buxton and beyond. Charlie Wardle, born in 1913, remembers 19 shops. Clive Wragg caps that with 27 when he was at school, though some of them not shops in the modern sense, but people selling from one room, like Miss Needham (p.75) and Jack Fearn.

It seems extraordinary that in Youlgrave there was a Co-op this size, selling, we must suppose, almost anything that people in the village and round about could need. However, in the heyday of the Co-op there were no supermarkets to compete and few people had cars.

The Co-op was founded in 1870 by Joseph Shimwell, Tom Birds and Joseph Smith, at first in Moor Lane. The present impressive building was erected in 1887 on a site where previously there had been a school for twenty-one poor children. From 1910 it supplied electricity and in 1920 was amalgamated with the Matlock Branch to form the Derwent Valley Co-operative Society Ltd. It stopped trading in 1968 and is now a Youth Hostel. Like many other buildings in the village it featured in the 1969 film version of D.H.Lawrence's story of *The Virgin and the Gypsy*.

In the Parish Magazine of 1926 it promised to supply ordered drapery and boots within seven to ten days. It also supplied 'groceries and provisions of the best quality', the price comparable 'with any house in the trade'. Tinned fruit and jam were a speciality.

Since the authors moved to the village a quarter of a century ago, many small businesses have closed.

Once there were small shops at the bottom of Bradford, near to the Farmyard Inn, in Fountain Square and the famous Beryl's, which sold almost everything - biscuits, tinned fruit, boot polish, cough mixture, clothes pegs and mousetraps. Not long ago there was a fish and chip shop. In addition there were travelling salesmen, selling anything from vegetables to paraffin. Prices seem absurd to us. Mrs Walker of Alport still has the details of payments to T Rowland in 1940. She paid 4d for a knob on the kettle lid.

Arnold Evans and his daughter Alice (Brassington) about 1929, outside his grocer's shop at the bottom of Moor Lane. The window appears to be decorated, perhaps for a carnival. Alice, then twelve, remembers that dress, which she loved, 'cream, edged with green'.

At various times this row of cottages in Main Street housed the post office, a shoe shop and a cobblers. Frank Evans repaired shoes and Mrs Evans sold them. His advertisement in the 1945 Trinity Methodist Jubilee booklet states, 'Boot and Shoe Dealer. Established over 100 years. All kinds of Repairs neatly executed.' There was at one time a cobbler working in Conksbury Lane, opposite the George, so Youlgrave people should have been well-shod. The house on Co-op Hill, opposite the bottom of Moor Lane, has housed a variety of businesses.

F. FEARN

Main Street
Youlgrave

Grocer and
Provision Dealer

Licensed to sell
Tobacco

B. BUXTON

Main Street
Youlgrave

FRUITERER
AND
CONFECTIONER

All Bread and
Confectionery
baked on our
own premises

Van
deliveries
daily

Est. 1903

A. BODEN & SONS

The Local Bakers and Confectioners

Church Street, Youlgrave

The Old Bakery was started by John 'Baker' Boden's father and mother, Abel and Lizzie, in 1903. Above is Mrs Lizzie Boden working in the bakery in the 1950s. It must be near Easter as she had just made hot X buns. 'Baker' Boden and his wife ran the bakery between 1971 and 1981. Abel and John both served as school governors and on the Parish Council, giving about 70 years of service to the village. Shown above, advertising in the Trinity Methodist Church Handbook of 1945.

The Old Bakery in a new guise,
providing accommodation.

Another shop to have changed use is Harry Hall's butcher's shop in Fountain Square.

Advertising in a 1966 parish magazine.
Fortunately through all these changes the post office, Parkers', Holland's and the paper shop thrive.

The post office before 1923 on the south side of Church Street. Then it was taken over by the Nuttall family and moved across the road to the present paper shop. James Fryer remembers going there with his grandfather and seeing the telephone kiosk inside. Later it moved to Main Street before settling conveniently in Fountain Square.

Parkers' shop early in the century with a Woodbine sign outside. The lady may be Mrs Finney since the Finneys had the shop before Fred Parker arrived after World War II.

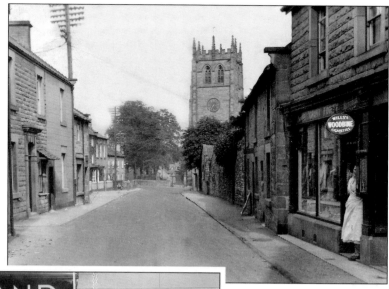

Holland's Butchers, now generally known as 'Figgies', in the early 1960s. The first refrigerated shop window in Youlgrave.

Harry Holland junior outside the shop with a prize bullock c.1960, with Irene watching from the doorway.

Down in Alport in the nineteenth century there were many trades and shops. In 1827 there was calico weaving, woollen weaving, a currier, and a woodturner as well as two doctors and a lawyer. In 1847 there was a little school at Dene Cottage, a weavers' shed in Walkers' stackyard, a brewhouse and the Old Cock Inn where Bridge House now stands. That was in the days of lead smelting.

By the beginning of the twentieth century Alport was quieter but Cyril Rowland remembers with pleasure Miss Needham's kitchen where she made humbugs. It is said that she was not overawed by anyone and turned away the potential custom of the Duke of Rutland on the grounds that if she sold to him there would not be enough for 'her Stanton lads'.

As the twentieth century progressed more and more visitors arrived. Once there was a teashop called Green Apple on Church Corner, since closed, but walkers and tourists are revived at Viv Butler's Meadow Cottage in Holywell Lane with its Teas with Hovis sign. It is removed during the winter and its reappearance, like the first swallows, is a sign of spring.

In the 20th century there was a diversity of industry in Youlgrave and Alport. Many buildings remain from activities long since abandoned. Quarrying and agriculture are still important. Many of the cottage industries have ceased but there was a time when Youlgrave was almost self-supporting. The increase in travel facilities, both private and public that came about after World War II, had a profound effect on village life. Among the new industries Asquith Associates, designers and silversmiths with workshops in Youlgrave, ran a thriving business for more than forty years. They had commissions from high places including the Royal Family and government. Tourism has also become important to the local economy with bed and breakfast premises and holiday cottages increasing in number.

In Lathkill Dale only a ruin remains of the structure built to house a Cornish beam engine in 1851.

Nothing now remains of the corn mill in Bradford Dale except a fragment of the engine house. In a sale schedule in 1895 it is part of a beautiful scene.

All that remains of the bobbin mill in Middleton Dale.

Alport Mill in 1980.

Raper Mine in 1970.

In the 1960s Charlie Bacon and Ken Brassington are seen shot firing at Raper opencast mine.

The site of Mawstone Mine in 1977. This lead mine was originally called "Shining Gutter". Abandoned for many years, after the World War I the Mawstone Mining Company was formed to work the mine. In May 1932 a disaster at the mine caused the death of eight men (see p.83). The mine is now derelict and capped.

The office building and lamp shed at Mawstone Mine in 1977.

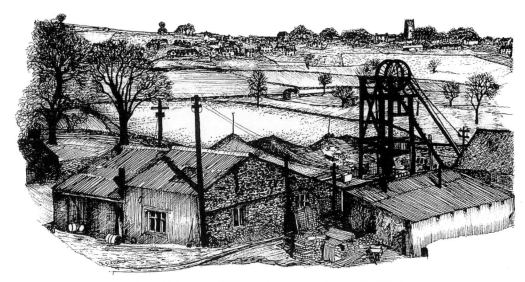

A drawing of Mawstone Mine as it may have looked in 1932.

An early picture of miners at Long Rake. 2nd from l, in the front row, is Joseph Francis Bacon.

A drawing of lead miners based on very old photographs.

This picture, probably taken in the 1930s, shows the sorting table at Long Rake. From the l: Jim Birds, Bernard Hadfield, ? .

Again the 1930s at Long Rake. Roger Wilson is in the centre at the back but we don't know who the others are.

Left: An early picture of the lead workings between Alport and Hawley's Bridge (note the lack of trees).

Below: A group of workers outside Friden Works in the early twentieth century. The overseer wears a collar and tie. We are told that if the workers were only a few minutes late, they were sent home with no pay.

Tom Birds working at Friden.

On 23 May 1932 an explosion in Mawstone Mine resulted in the instant deaths of five miners. These were William Brindley (22), John Gallagher (23), Geoffrey Gould (28), Poultney Porter (57), and his son James Porter (27). In a very brave attempt to rescue their workmates John Eric Evans (23), John William Birds (24) and mine manager Kenneth Seville (34) also died. Contemporary newspaper reports described the rescue attempt as "heroism without parallel in the history of British mining disasters." The inquest failed to establish the cause of the explosion conclusively but it is generally believed that firedamp had built up and was ignited by a spark from a fan. All the men, with the exception of the two Porters, were buried in Youlgrave churchyard.

Below: Mr. Poultney Porter and his son James, both victims of the disaster. They are buried near Penrith.

A contemporary press cutting describing the disaster.

Mr Seville died trying to rescue his men – he is said to have made three attempts to save them. His tombstone in the churchyard is inscribed: "In loving memory of Kenneth A Seville, late Managing Director of Mawstone Mines Ltd., who lost his life in the mine disaster May 23, 1932, in an endeavour to save that of his men".

Water was first piped into Youlgrave in 1829 from a spring at Mawstone. This came about mainly through the efforts of the Friendly Society of Women led by Miss Hannah Bowman. The water was brought to the Fountain (see p.62) from which the villagers drew water each morning – for this they paid an annual subscription of 6d. In 1869 a new scheme supplied water to taps in various parts of the village. This was funded by various benefactors including Thomas Smith of Manchester (a former resident), W P Thornhill of Stanton and the Duke of Rutland. Each man in the village agreed to pay the cost of at least three days labour. In order to pay the final bill the old iron pipes were sold and a short play called *The Evergreen Chit-Chat* written and produced by Mrs Susan Shimwell, was performed in the Reading Room. In 1919 there were great celebrations to mark the fiftieth anniversary of the second water undertaking – sadly no photographs of this event have come to light. In 1928 the supply was augmented by a second spring. In 1929 the centenary of the Waterworks was celebrated and the festivities included the presentation of a Centenary Mug (one of these was bought at Arundel in Sussex fairly recently and returned to the village). The Mawstone Mine explosion caused a fracture to the main supply pipe for which compensation was given by the Mining Company. The severe winter of 1963 caused extensive damage to pipes. In 1965 the water rate was raised to a realistic level. Ongoing problems at Coldwell End were solved by a pumping system installed in the Pinfold in 1972. In 1979 the 150th anniversary of the Waterworks was celebrated and a souvenir model of the Fountain was made by a local potter. Since 1979 the Waterworks has

weathered various problems and succeeded in maintaining the supply. A new supply has been found in the old Mawstone Mine and in times of severe drought the supply can be augmented by Severn Trent Water. The most recent crisis was in part brought about by the terrorist attack in the USA on 11th September 2001. It became extremely difficult to insure small organizations such as the Waterworks and for a short time it seemed that the company would have to be absorbed by Severn Trent Water. However, this problem was solved and we hope that the Waterworks will continue to supply the village for generations to come.

This is the original spring of 1829.

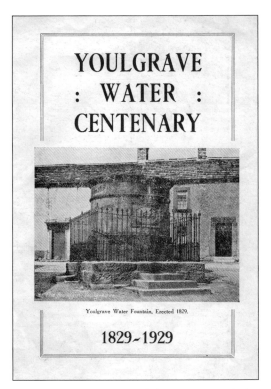

YOULGRAVE
: WATER :
CENTENARY

Youlgrave Water Fountain, Erected 1829.

1829~1929

The programme for the celebrations to mark the centenary of the Waterworks in 1929.

In c. 1952 Charlie Wardle (l.) and Joe Oldfield are seen mending a burst pipe in Stoneyside.

In the late 1980s a new pipe was laid. In this photograph the village can be seen in the distance. From the l: Dougie Oldfield, ? (not from Youlgrave), Bob Skinner, John Wardle, Sid Birds, Charlie Wardle and Roger Bacon.

Above: In 1986/7 Bob Skinner, then manager of the Waterworks, stands outside the Bull's Head with a glass of Youlgrave water.

Bob Skinner inspecting the spring at Bleakley Wood.

In the 1990s, John Wardle is seen at the original spring in Bleakley Wood....

....And at the modern installations.

Farming has been an important part of life in Youlgrave and Alport for centuries and continues to be so. There has been some diversification with buildings being converted into holiday accommodation and fields becoming caravan and camping sites. Various epidemics of foot and mouth disease and BSE have taken their toll. However, life goes on.

These thatched haystacks were somewhere near Alport Mill in the early 1900s.

Mr Mosley's cattle making their way through Alport in the 1940s.

Feeding chickens in Alport in 1945. Isobel Bailey (née Mosley) tells us that the hollow ash tree in the background was burned down by a picnicker's fire. She can recollect the sound of the Bakewell fire engine's bell.

Joe Shimwell at Anniscroft Farm in the 1960s.

Ezra and Joe Shimwell at Bakewell Market in the 1950s.

On this haywagon in the 1930s Luther Shimwell is on top of the load. Joseph Shimwell is on the left and Ezra Shimwell is holding the horse.

Tom Walker bred shire horses at Alport in the 1940s. Harry Holland is on the left.

There was great consternation at Anniscroft Farm when a hay barn burned down in the 1930s.

In the 1950s Harry Holland was pictured with his pig – called Alice apparently!

William Dakin Shimwell cutting grass on Spardles before World War II. The horse-drawn mower had revolutionary rubber tyres and the cutter bar was driven by a petrol engine.

Hay-making on Spardles before World War II. From l: Daniel Prime, John Birds, William Dakin Shimwell and Luther Shimwell on top of the load.

Anthony, Noel and Tom Walker scything in 1926.

Hay-making during World War I.

Early in the 1930s Noel Walker gave some hikers a ride in his horse-drawn cart.

Sheepshearing in the early 1930s.

Laying out sheared fleeces.

In the early 1950s a tractor overturned down Bradford. Spectators included John
Stevenson and Sid Birds.

An ancient trackway, the Portway, runs through Alport, mediaeval saltways and packhorse bridges abound in the area, but even with the coming of tarmac roads, traffic in Youlgrave would have been light. Cottages like those in Bankside did not need parking. Carts passed through as tractors do now, but lorries and buses were not a problem.

Gentle traffic round about 1900. Dr Greenhough's pony and trap.

About thirty years later, James Fryer and his grandfather outside Old Hall Farm.

Two pleasant ways to get about. The lady is Miss Birds, later Mrs Harrison, pictured in 1913 with her motorcycle. Of the children with bicycles, the boy is identified as John Brindley.

The earliest cars in the village would hardly have caused a traffic problem, though they probably caused some excitement and pride to their owners. Harry Holland and Cliff Ledger showing off an MG in Holland's Croft in the 1930s.

Charlie Wardle says that his father Arthur's Model T Ford was one of only three in Youlgrave in the 1920s, the other two belonging to Arthur Marsden and Reggie Garratt. In the picture on the right, it stands outside his shop, now Church Farm. The sign states clearly Wardle, Motor Proprietor.

R 8750 was sometimes used as a taxi. It is thought that the two ladies were Mrs and Miss Evans, on their way to Rowsley railway station.

The George with its mounting block recalls traditional methods of transport. A horse and trap is going down Conksbury Lane. On the wall is the Midland Railway timetable along with the sign telling us that the George was once a Midland Railway Parcel Receiving Office. To the right of the George is Wardle's shop, now Church Farm, around 1914. It is advertising Colman's starch. This is a splendidly evocative picture of old Youlgrave.

Two pictures of young drivers. Irene Holland (now Shimwell), on the left, learned to drive in a Ford Prefect in the late 1960s, Joan Shimwell and Hilda Moss standing by.

On the right is Michael Shimwell with the MG bought with his 21st birthday gifts.

Lorries and buses became more common. The bus above was having trouble on Alport Hill in the 1960s and needed a tow from Shimwells' milk lorry.

HULLEY'S MOTOR (Summer) SERVICE

Between Chesterfield, Old Brampton, Wadshelf, Baslow, Pilsley (for Edensor and Chatsworth), Bakewell, Alport, Youlgrave.   Parties Catered for Long Day Tours.   Charas & Taxis for Hire.   Haulage.

Hy. Hulley & Sons, Derwent Garage, Baslow. Tel. Baslow 46.

DAILY SERVICE.

		a.m.	a.m.	a.m.	p.m.	p.m.	p.m.	p.m.	p.m.	p.m.
Chesterfield	dep.	8-15	10-0	11-30	2-0	3-30	5-15	6-15	8-0	9-0
Old Brampton	,,	8-30	10-15	11-45	2-15	3-45	5-30	6-30	8-15	9-15
Wadshelf	,,	8-40	10-25	11-55	2-25	3-55	5-40	6-40	8-25	9-25
Baslow	,,	9-0	10-50	12-20	2-50	4-20	6-0	7-5	8-40	9-50
Pilsley	,,	9-10	11-0	12-30	3-0	4-30	6-10	7-15	8-50	
Bakewell	,,	9-20	11-10	12-40	3-10	4-40	6-20	7-25	9-0	
Youlgrave	arr.	9-40		1-5	3-30			7-45		

		a.m.	a.m.	a.m.	p.m.	p.m.	p.m.	p.m.	p.m.	p.m.
Youlgrave	dep.			9-40		1-30	3-40		7-45	
Bakewell	,,			10-0	12-25	2-0	4-0	5-0	7-0	8-0	9-0
Pilsley	,,			10-10	12-35	2-10	4-10	5-10	7-10	8-10	9-10
Baslow	,,	7-30	9-0	10-20	12-45	2-20	4-20	5-20	7-20	8-20	9-20
Wadshelf	,,	7-45	9-20	10-40	1-5	2-40	4-40	5-40	7-35	8-35	
Old Brampton	,,	7-55	9-30	10-50	1-15	2-50	4-50	5-50	7-45	8-45	
Chesterfield	arr.	8-15	9-50	11-10	1-30	3-10	5-10	6-10	8-0	9-0	

SUNDAY SERVICE.

		p.m.	p.m.	p.m.	p.m.	p.m.	p.m.	p.m.	p.m.
Chesterfield	dep.	11-30	2-30	3-30		6-15	8-0	9-0	10-15
Old Brampton	,,	11-45	2-45	3-45		6-30	8-15	9-15	10-30
Wadshelf	,,	11-55	2-55	3-55		6-45	8-25	9-25	10-40
Baslow	,,	12-20	3-20	4-20	5-40	7-5	8-40	9-50	11-0
Pilsley	,,	12-30	3-30	4-30	5-50	7-15	8-50		
Bakewell	,,	12-40	3-40	4-40	6-0	7-25	9-0		
Youlgrave	arr.		4-0		6-20	7-45			

		p.m.	p.m.	p.m.	p.m.	p.m.	p.m.	p.m.	p.m.
Youlgrave	dep.			4-0			6-40	7-45	
Bakewell	,,		1-0		4-20	5-0	7-0	8-0	9-0
Pilsley	,,		1-10		4-30	5-10	7-10	8-10	9-10
Baslow	,,	10-20	1-20	2-20	4-40	5-20	7-20	8-20	9-20
Wadshelf	,,	10-40	1-40	2-40		5-40	7-35	8-35	9-40
Old Brampton	,,	10-50	1-50	2-50		5-50	7-45	8-45	9-55
Chesterfield	arr.	11-10	2-10	3-10		6-10	8-0	9-0	10-10

EXTRA BUSES SATURDAY.

		a.m.	p.m.	p.m.	p.m.	p.m.	p.m.	p.m.
Chesterfield	dep.	10-0	12-30	1-0	4-20	5-15	9-0	10-15
Old Brampton	,,	10-15		1-15	4-35	5-30	9-15	10-30
Wadshelf	,,	10-25	1-0	1-25	4-45	5-45	9-25	10-40
Baslow	,,	10-50				6-0	9-50	11-0
Pilsley	,,	11-0				6-10	10-0	
Bakewell	,,	11-10*				6-20	10-10	
Youlgrave	arr.	11-30*				6-40	10-30	

		a.m.	p.m.	p.m.	p.m.	p.m.	p.m.	p.m.
Youlgrave	dep.		12-0* noon		6-40		10-30	
Bakewell	,,		12-25		7-0	9-0	10-45	
Pilsley	,,		12-35		7-10	9-10	10-55	
Baslow	,,	9-30	12-45		7-20	9-20	11-0	
Wadshelf	,,	9-50	1-5	1-30	7-35	9-40		
Old Brampton	,,	10-0	1-15	1-40	7-45	9-55		
Chesterfield	arr.	10-15	1-30	1-55	8-0	10-10		

(*)—Runs Saturday and Monday only.

FARES.	Single.	Return.
Chesterfield to Youlgrave	2/6	4/3
,, Bakewell	1/9	3/-
,, Baslow	1/3	2/-
Bakewell to Youlgrave	9d.	1/3

DEPOTS.
Chesterfield: Markham Road.
Baslow: Church & Derwent Garage.
Bakewell: The Square.
Youlgrave: George Hotel.

The Proprietors are not responsible for loss of time or detention from any cause whatever.

The bus timetable from the Parish Magazine in 1926. There were 9 buses on weekdays. The fare from Chesterfield to Youlgrave was 2/6 single, 4/3 return; the fare to Bakewell was 9d and 1/3. Hulleys even then were offering day tours and charabanc and taxi hire.

Margaret Folley recalls that girls from Youlgrave and Alport, working at Friden during World War I, walked there. However, in 1922 Wooliscrofts started a service from Alport to Friden and Mrs Folley was the first to travel on it from Alport.

This Commer lorry, one of only 15 manufactured, pictured in front of the Old Hall Farm round about 1930, carried 17 and 12 gallon churns of milk to Manchester daily.

A more up-to-date vehicle in 1983, with Michael, Dakin, Hannah and Marjorie Shimwell.

Cars, buses and charabancs needed fuel. Here, c.1950, James Fryer, Peter Prince and Michael Ilott stand in front of the Youlgrave garage. It was built in 1928 and originally was called Evans and Prince.

At one time the Farmyard sold petrol, the pumps across the road from the main building. John Brindley, Mena Harrison and another stand outside the garage in 1933.

As traffic increased, the Boarding House Hotel (p.62 and p.139) on Alport Hill became a problem as the road beside it was narrow and on a sharp bend.

In the left-hand photograph the open-topped vehicle from Sheffield has a tight turn to negotiate. Isobel Bailey (née Mosley) recalls how her mother, returning from church to Lathkill House Farm, expected to find cyclists in the trees in the middle of the picture above. So the road had to be straightened and widened and the hotel demolished.

When the Hotel was demolished c. 1937 and the road widened, so too was Alport Bridge, shown above before widening.

There has long been great enthusiasm for sport in the village. As well as the traditional team games like cricket and football, we now have a flourishing *boules* team. Badminton is played regularly in the village hall and tennis on the courts at the playing field. There is a well-established bowls club which started almost 70 years ago. In the past there have been keep-fit classes (for the ladies, apparently). And now there are yoga and *t'ai chi* classes. There has been a homing pigeon society for many years. And the pubs have enthusiastic darts teams that play in local leagues. But the greatest claim to fame must be made by the great All Saints' Tug of War team that established Youlgrave as national champions in their sport in the 1960s and 70s.

Tug-Of-War

Tug-of-War became popular in the village following the 1966 and 1967 carnivals. The team was originally called 'Nab's Lads', after the trainer Albert 'Nab' Oldfield, or the 'Bull's Head team', after the pub frequented by some of the members. Later they named themselves after All Saints' Church. The club was able to make up seven teams, from 88-stone to 180-stone. In 1969, the 88-stone team won its class in the National Indoor Tug-of-War Championships, as did the 108-stone team and the Youth team. But in 1970 All Saints' became the first teams ever to win all national events at Crystal Palace. Other successes followed until eventually Nabby emigrated to Australia and some of the team members had other commitments. But the remaining members decided to amalgamate with Sheen and the resulting team went on to represent England successfully in both Euro-pean and World championships.

The newspapers reported All Saints' suc-cess with great enthusiasm: 'The mighty mus-cled men of Youlgreave made tug-of-war history....when they became national cham-pions at all five weights at Crystal Palace. Nobody has pulled together with such strength and success in the sport's history.'

'Britain's top indoor tug o' war champions, the Youlgreave All Saints' team who domi-nated the season's tug of war scene....'

Youlgrave All Saints' training in c.1970 with their 'secret weapon' - a 15 cwt. cement, lead and chain filled barrel on a pulley between two former telegraph poles. From the right: M Stacey, G Webster, 'Biffo' Brindley, T Evans, T Bacon, C Webster, T Carter, H Barton, M Roland and their coach Mr Albert 'Nabby' Oldfield.

The Junior team with their trophies outside the George Hotel. Back row from the left: Guy Webster, Mick Andrews, Eddie Oldfield, ?, ?; front row: Don Stacey, Martin Fryer, Mick Rowland, Vincent Webster, Peter Brindley, Michael Shimwell, Trevor Bacon, Roger Elliott, ?, ?, Paul Weller, Malcolm Stacey.

In 1969 some of his team-mates attempted to 'hang' Michael Shimwell outside Nabby Oldfield's house. From the left: Mick Andrews, Don Stacey, Malcolm Stacey.

1967/8. Miss Derbyshire, Leslie McRindle, presents the winners' trophy to Nabby Oldfield. Brian Frost is on the extreme right with Eddie Shimwell just behind him. Apparently, at this moment, the beer barrel was still full.

As well as playing sports in the village, Youlgrave boys also did well in teams at Lady Manners School.

In this Lady Manners' rugby team in the 1950s Michael Shimwell is 2nd from the left on the back row and Colin Brassington is 6th. On the front row: 3rd from the left is Robert Walker, 5th Albert Hall and 7th David Needham.

A Lady Manners' cricket team in 1967 has five Youlgrave boys in it. On the back row, from the left: 1st Carl Richardson, 3rd Dennis Marsden, 4th Chris Shimwell, 5th Derek Dunn. On the front row, 2nd from the right: Nick Asquith.

Cricket

Cricket has a long history in Youlgrave - the club celebrated its centenary in June 1971. Around the turn of the century an old railway carriage was used as a pavilion and there was no proper wicket. In the early days the team travelled to away matches by horse and cart. The team reformed after World War I but there was still no proper wicket. Some fine players came to prominence, notably Colin Gregory described as 'the finest fast bowler ever to walk on to the Youlgrave pitch'. Charlie Botham is another legendary player who can be seen as umpire in one of the photographs. After the Second World War a good team was formed but in the 1950s various problems occurred and eventually the team moved to Friden in 1969. In 1971 the Club returned to the village into a newly-built pavilion. Since then the Club has had a chequered history. However, we look forward to the future and wish the players every success.

This team played Ashford on 1 September 1934 and won 91-62.

In 1993 Youlgrave played a match against a Derbyshire XI. A new score box was opened in memory of Peter Hill who was killed by lightning while umpiring a cricket match in May 1992.

A 1955 cricket team. Back row from the left: Greg Hadfield, Harold Bacon, John Dale, Ted Craw, Sam Allen, Bert Evans, Ivor Hayes, Frank Evans, Henry Carson, Charles Botham (umpire), Ernest Shimwell (scorer); front row from the left: Hugo Waterhouse, Harold Hadfield, Jack Rowland, Maurice Wagstaffe, Tom Craw, Harold Wragg.

A team in the early 90s. Back row, from the left: Nick Kirkland, Tom Marvin, James Allen, Andrew Walker, Peter Hill, Dominic Asquith; front row, from the left: Mark Walker, Nick Asquith, Robert Jackson, Robert Allen, David Askew (?).

Football

Football has a long and distinguished history in Youlgrave. We have seen a photograph of a team taken on the vicarage lawn in about 1890. Over the years there have been many successes as the various pictures of cup-winning teams show. The Junior teams in particular have done well, especially in recent years.

An early football team.

A Youlgrave football team that played against Matlock Town in 1948.

In 1920 Youlgrave won the Moxon Cup.

Youlgrave United Reserves won the Roden Cup in 1982.

The Junior football team in 1998. Back row from the left: David Figg, Tony Figg, Anthony Wragg; third: Daniel Butterworth, Jonathon Figg, Joe Hurford, George Wood, Jeremy Bourne, John Simpson; second: James Wood, Jean-Marc Randon, Thomas Rhodes, Scott Andrews, David Wragg; front: Matthew Simpson, Jack Stacey, Michael Hope, Eric Johnson.

Youlgrave Football Club 1926-7. This was a very distinguished team. They were champions of Matlock and District Senior League, winners of the Wirksworth Charity Cup and runners-up in the Derbyshire Divisional Cup and the Cavendish Cup. On the back row (as printed on the photograph), from the left: J Lomas (trainer), F Wilson, B Hambleton, C Wigley, S Wardle, A Hambleton, R Pilkington, H Wardle (vice-captain), G Housley, F Dawson, E Bowing (*this should be Bowring*). The front row: B Billings (*this should be Billinge*), A Wardle, G W Gimber (Capt), F Spooner, T F Wardle, R Moody, G H Ollerenshaw (Asst Sec), J Brindley, Jnr.

The Youlgrave Homing Society was founded about eighty years ago. In this picture, taken in the Bull's Head in the 1990s, Michael Wragg (left), secretary of the Society for around 30 years, is seen shaking hands with the current president David Shimwell.

In 1988 the Homing Society organised a sponsored walk to raise funds. Some young supporters outside the George Hotel after the walk are, from the left: Cassie Shimwell, Martin Shimwell, Lee Webster with brother Barry behind him, and Andrew Colman.

In 2000, during a race from Nantes in France, seven pigeons mistakenly landed on the Q E II while it was docked in Southampton. Five disappeared but two travelled to New York (via the Caribbean) and back. Vince Webster went to collect his bird, subsequently named Liberty, at Southampton. Vince is shown with Liberty outside his loft on Stoneyside after Liberty's safe return.

Youlgrave Homing Society Ladies' Bowling Team. From the left: Helen Webster, Annette Shimwell, ? Bateman, Karen Nuttall, Jean Shimwell, Sandra Poole, Mick Partridge (looking perturbed).

Tennis

Youlgrave Tennis Club was started in the early 1980s. Gill Pickworth, Sue Barradell and John Pickworth are seen relaxing between games at the tennis courts.

Keeping Fit

Ladies' Keep-Fit class in 1969. Back row, from the left: Francis Bacon, Barbara Asquith, Pam Nuttall, Loretta Ince, Cynthia Billingham, Maria ?, Jenny Calhoun; front row: ? , Lyn Burgess, Ann Armitt, Margaret Grant.

Another Keep-Fit class, this time during World War II, at the top Chapel Girls' Club. Ida Smith is in the middle, with her piano on the trailer in the background. The girls are, back row, from the left: Lilian Thompson, Peggy Thompson, Barbara Oldfield and Katherine Twyford; middle row: Eileen Thompson, Eileen Brassington, Valerie Birds; front row: Barbara Thompson, Dorothy Twyford, Ann Robinson, Cynthia Hall.

The village has always had darts teams, regularly taking part in local league competitions. It was reported that, in May 1957, the Youlgrave and District Darts League held their annual dinner at the George Hotel. It was attended by about 80 people. The Bull's Head Hotel won the Doubles competition and also the Landlord's Cup. Individual winners included Mr H Oldfield (George Hotel), Mr A Oldfield (Knoll Club) and Mr J Purseglove (Bull's Head).

The George Hotel Ladies' Darts team in 1980. Back row from the left: Ethel Wilson, Glenys Bristow, Betty Wilson, Margaret Smedley; front row: Linda Andrews, Sylvia Brindley (landlady), Chris Carnell, Margaret Birds.

John Lowe, who was World Darts Champion in the 1970s and 80s, is seen here with the George Hotel players in 1978. From the left: Vince Webster, John Kilbride, David Kenworthy, Guy Webster, Geoff Andrews, John Lowe, Peter Smedley, Bruce Webster, Peter Kilbride, Ray Purseglove, Glyn Bristow, Gordon Coupe.

The Bowls Club started about 70 years ago. It was suspended during World War II and was not re-established until 1975 (by Derek Oldfield, Leslie Harley and Frank Oldfield). In 2000 a new pavilion was built with funds from the National Lottery. The Bowls Club originally organised the Carnival as a means of raising money.

In the mid-1990s, from the left: Diane Harrison (née Oldfield), Richard Swindell, Robert Dawson, Martin Harrison.

From the left: David Upton, Frank Harrison, Derek Oldfield, Wilfred Elliott.

In complete contrast, people are seen playing croquet at Lathkill House Farm in Alport in 1938.

Chapter 13 – A Variety of Societies

Youlgrave Scouts was formed in 1910 with the Rev. Greenshields as the first Scoutmaster. It proved to be very popular as can be seen in the many happy photographs taken in the early years. At the time of writing there are Venture Scouts in the village, but no ordinary Scout, Cub or Beaver Packs. Hopefully these will start again. For the girls, Rangers, Guides and Brownies were joined by the Rainbows in 1991.

Other groups in the village include the Women's Institute (founded in 1919), the Darby and Joan Club, the Women's Fellowship, the Monday Club, the Horticultural Society, the Christian Fellowship, the Sunday Club (formerly Sunday School) and the Young People's Fellowship.

Scouts

The Scouts and Cubs after a church parade in 1935.

The Rev. Greenshields saluting in the early days of Youlgrave Scouts.

Scouts giving each other a helping hand while shaving at an early camp.

George Holland and Ezra Toft in the early 1920s.

The Scouts' pantomime in 1979.

Charlie Wardle and Bill Shimwell, probably in Llandudno, before World War II.

A merry band of Scouts. Back row from l: Hollis Fraser, Len Taylor, Frank Evans, Reg Cawley. Middle row: Harold Wardle, Tom Craw, Charlie Wardle. Front: Bill Slaney, Jack Brassington.

A dinner of the Youlgrave Baden Powell Guild of Old Scouts at the George Hotel in the 1960s. Seated from l: Cyril Upchurch, Harry Goodwin, Norman Wilson, R W P Cockerton, Ernest Johnson, Eric Billinge. Standing from l: Albert Shimwell, Eric Shimwell, Norman Bacon, Roger Bacon, John Twyford, Chris Toft.

We *think* this may have been during the celebrations of King George V's Jubilee. There is a union flag flying at Wardle's shop in the background.

The Guides at Well Dressing in the 1950s. Among them can be seen Miss McComb, Christine Shimwell, Kath Gilbert, Susan Brassington, Dorothy Gilbert, Wendy Bosley, Hilary Birds, Valerie Clark and Pearl Webster.

The Guides in about 1956.

In 1957 the Guides attended the first 4-yearly international camp at Chatsworth. Not all the girls in this picture are from Youlgrave. Back row from l: 1st Joan McComb (head teacher of the infant school), 4th Mary Elliott, 5th Kath Gilbert, 8th Pam Clark, 9th Hilary Mills, 10th Mary Purseglove. Middle row: 1st Merle Cawley, 2nd Chris Shimwell, 7th Sybil Shimwell, 9th Dorothy Gilbert, 10th Pearl Webster. Front row: 1st Kate Elliott, 2nd Brenda Upton, 3rd Hilary Birds, 4th Dorothy Elliott with Annette Bosley right behind her, Yvonne Wilson, ?, Val Clark, Viv Wragg, Susan Brassington.

Left: In the 1980s the Guides are seen in school writing to various VIPs for donations towards their Adopt and Cherish garden project. At the back l: Genevieve Wilson. Front: Laura Knowles, Susie Pearson, Sue Lomas (Guider), Helen Taylor.

Right: Dawn Gladwin, Helen Taylor and Claire Gibling preparing bulbs for planting in the Adopt and Cherish garden.

Below: Guides receiving an award for the Adopt and Cherish project in the 1980s. Standing from l: ?, Fiona Mallaband, ?, Teresa Oldfield, Helen Taylor, Claire Walker, Gillian Gibling, Jane Ardley, Claire Gibling, Susanna Bacon, Emma Wherret (just visible), ?, Kneeling: Molly Prince with, behind her, ?. Kirsty Gow. Kneeling on the r., ?, Charlotte Town, Claire Harmon.

The Brownies in the 1990s. From l: ?, Kerry Oldfield, Briony Harrison, Lucianne Marshall.

Rangers in about 1980. From the l: Carole Oldfield, Anne Purseglove, Diane Oldfield, Fiona Bowes, Janice Wilson, Katy Baker.

After World War II the W. I. celebrated the advent of peace with a pageant. Back row from l: Mrs Ted Lomas, Mrs Ollerenshaw, Mrs Bertha Frost, Mrs Marjorie Shimwell, Mrs Laurence Birds, Mrs Ida Smith. Front row: Kathleen Toft, Mrs Elsie Lomas, Mrs Dick Ogden.

The W.I. went on a visit to Wedgewood at Barlaston. Among those present were: Mrs Keyworth, Mrs H Shimwell, Mrs Boardman, Ann Robinson, Connie Holland, Lucy Wardle, Mrs Weston, Mrs Wild, Mrs L Scriven, Mrs M Birds, Mrs Dale, Mrs Hall, Miss Purseglove, Mrs Costello, Mrs K Twyford, Alice Brassington, Mrs G Clark, Mrs M Purseglove, Mrs Gladys Sheldon, Mrs Mills, Mrs Mary Needham, Mrs Marjorie Shimwell, Mrs J Dale, Mrs J Cawley, Mrs Lees, Mrs Hewitt, Margaret Fell, Mrs Lomas, Mrs Martha Purseglove.

W.I. ladies outside the Farmyard at carnival time.

Darby and Joan

The Darby and Joan Club started in 1957 and met at the Bulls' Head for many years before moving to the Village Hall.

This is an outing in the early years. Among those present were: Mr Wheeldon, Mr and Mrs V Wilson, Mrs M Purseglove, Mrs Kenworthy, Mrs J Evans, Mrs D Thompson, Mrs C Brassington, Mrs Purseglove, Mr Dunn, Mrs C Twyford, Mrs Walker, Gladys Sheldon, Mrs M Birds, Mrs E Shimwell, Mrs Mary Needham, Mr Wood, Miss Slaney, Mrs F Wilson, Mr Oldfield, Mrs Dunn, Mrs M Lomas, Mrs Slaney, Mrs Wheeldon, Mrs Hewitt, Mrs Wood, Mrs Warrington, Mrs Scarborough and others.

The pantomime is a very important date in Youlgrave's calendar and a major component of Village Hall funding. It is looked forward to and attended by people from far and wide. Several performances are sold out well in advance. The show runs for two weeks and there is a very popular matinée on the first Saturday. As well as the cast there is a large team of backstage workers who build scenery, sew costumes, sell ice creams, programmes and tickets.

In 1927 Major Mockett, manager of the Village Hall, produced *Dick Whittington* which ran for six performances. He produced two other pantomimes. In 1962 Norman Wilson revived the pantomime with *Babes in the Wood,* an instant success. After five years, Norman was followed consecutively by producers Martin Brooke-Taylor, Margaret Fell, Stephen Walker and John Roper. In 1977 Jan Wilson, Norman's wife, began a long and successful period as producer and musical director and continues in both roles now. She had two years off in 1998 and 1999 when the show was directed by Louise Page and Chris Hawes.

A performance of (we think) *Puss in Boots* in the 1920s.

We think this is Major Mockett's production of *Cinderella,* some time in the 1920s. Front row: Margaret Bateman, Dorothy Harrison, Ena Bibby, Joan Marsden, Cynthia Marsden, Elsie Ogden; back row: Mary Birds, Marjorie Rose, Mr Coleman, Mr Bernard Hadfield, Jack Rowland, Jim Birds, Alice Bacon, Eileen Marsden, Joyce Elsom (?), Mary Evans, Nellie Thompson; at the back: Norman Brassington and Bob Rowland.

Tom 'Mighty Fine' Rhodes and David Pryor in *The Queen of Hearts* in 1980.

Behind the scenes at the 1962 production of *Babes in the Woods*. From the left: Robert Young (now the florist), Vivian Wragg and Harry Sandell.

Babes in the Woods 1962. From the left: Mary Goodwin, Susan Wigglesworth, Corinna Wragg, Hilary Mills, Christine Bosley, Avril Fryer, Jean Wragg, Susan Lomas.

Ann Slaney in one of Major Mockett's productions in 1928.

Ann Slaney in 1929.

And again, in 1929.

Babes in the Woods 1962. From the left: Mary Witham (née Hall), Norman Wilson (the producer), Vivian Wragg.

Dorothy Sandell (wardrobe) and Jan Wilson (producer) in conference in 1977.

At a rehearsal in the 1960s. Isabel Mosley (though she says it isn't!), Colin Brassington, with Mrs Ida Smith (née Bacon) at the piano.

John Roper, Chris Carnell and Tom Rhodes in *Sleeping Beauty* in 1978. Jack Goodwin and David Brown were inside the horse!

The cast of *Robinson Crusoe* in 1977.

From the left: Mary Lievesley, Trudy Nuttall, Susan Carson and Chris Carnell in *Cinderella* in 1979.

The cast of *Cinderella* in 1979.

1982. Mrs Horton at the piano with the Seven Dwarves in *Snow White*. From the left: Kirsty Gow, Ēilis Hague, Michael Wherrett, Cassie Worth, John Hague, Ralph Wilson and Adrian Wragg.

From the left: Ray Rippingale, Simon Frost and Jack Elliott in *Robinson Crusoe* in 1994.

Rumpelstiltskin in 1986. Back row, from the left: Elizabeth Ede, Ann Pickworth, Nicholas Stacey, Hannah Shimwell; front from the left: Ellen Rhodes, Jenny Osborne, Sarah Edge.

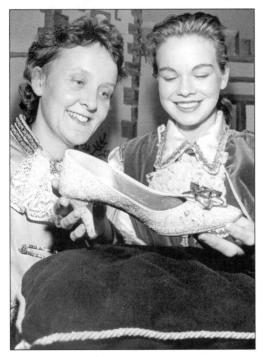

Ann Croasdell and Hannah Shimwell in *Cinderella* in 1991.

From the left: Mick Partridge and Phil Wildbore in *Cinderella* in 1991.

Carnival has a long history in Youlgrave. It is said that it was started in 1932 by Youlgrave Bowls Club but we have found photographs of earlier events. The Carnival does not take place every year. When it does, the Committee usually organises a week of fun ending with the grand procession on Saturday. Often there is a disco with live music on Saturday night. For some of the following photographs we have not been able to get definite dates and names, but we're sure you will recognise yourselves and your relations!

No date for this one, but from the look of the lorry, it is obviously quite early.

Margaret Webster as Carnival Queen in the 1920s. Major Mockett (manager of the village hall and producer of pantomimes) is on the extreme left and next to him are Mr and Mrs Potter who lived in the Old Hall at the time (and may have been judges). On the dray Mary Needham is on the left and Betty Wilson is next to her. Elsie Ogden is standing next to Queen Margaret and we don't know who the little girl is!

'Gypsies' in the 1950s.

An interesting float in the 1951 carnival.

A fine line-up of majorettes about 40 years ago. From the left: Noreen Ludlum, Jane Birds, Norma Stone, Mary Holland, Avril Smith, Ann Webster, Freda Webster, Lyn ?, Christine Oldfield, Carol Stone.

In the carnival of 1949, a number of women dressed as a male football team and men dressed as women. Here are the ladies – unfortunately (or perhaps fortunately) we do not have a photograph of the men!

In the 1950s Fred Whitmore and Harry Sandell did a double act as 'Slap and Dash'.

Carnival Queen Hilda Elliott is crowned by the Rev Hadfield and his daughter Jean.

For a carnival in the 1920s a float was prepared in Old Hall Farm yard. Reginald Evans and his father Arthur are standing by.

The regulars from the George Hotel took up morris dancing for this carnival.

Perhaps those boys from the George should have kept up the morris dancing. Here they are seen as the 'Launderettes'.

Queens past and present — grandmother Evelyn Bristow, left, with daughter Lorna Rogers, right, and granddaughter Jayne Bristow.

Queen Jayne on the family throne

By Janice Mullin

Evelyn when she was 1938 carnival queen.

In 1980, Jayne Bristow became the third generation in her family to be chosen as Youlgrave Carnival Queen. Her mother Lorna was Queen in 1965 and her grandmother Evelyn in 1938.

HOLLANDS HAGGIS HUNTERS

In 1983 Holland's Haggis Hunters celebrate a local shop's popular product.

Margaret Thatcher and Michael Foot buried the hatchet in order to attend Youlgrave carnival in 1983.

WOT! NO PAVILION THE PARISH COUNCIL SAY "NOT ENOUGH DOUGH"

YOULGRAVE UNITED

A float refers to a dispute over the pavilion on the Playing Fields in the late 1960s.

In the 1930s Arthur Evans (left) and Miriam Fryer won first prize as Past and Present Mill Girls.

Young Michael Shimwell as a tramp in the 1950s.

Above: At a carnival in the 1930s the Queen is Frances Yates attended by Margaret Boardman (back l.), Margaret Hadfield (front l.), Janet Marsden (back r.) and Mary Hall (front r.).

Left: Villagers enjoying a carnival in the 1930s.

A picture of carnival entrants in the 1920s, outside the Reading Room. We believe that the lady (?) in the middle is Bernard Hadfield and the man in dark glasses is Dan Prime.

These may be members of the Oldfield family enjoying a carnival in the 1920s.

In this photograph of the 1935 carnival Marie Evans (née Wardle) is seen as Miss Youlgrave.

The Pommie Moonrakers outside the Bull's Head in the 1950s. Among them are: Ellis Bowring, Harry Goodwin, Harry Oldfield, Ellis Birds, John Mellor, Bob Skinner, Charlie Birds, Hugh Ollerenshaw, Ron Brown, Frank Twyford, Jack Goodwin, Alan Oldfield, Harry Hall, Derek Lomas and others.

A carnival band on the playing field before World War II. Charlie Wardle has the small drum and Harold Wragg the big one.

Youlgrave and Alport like an excuse to celebrate.

In 1953 a large number of children enjoyed a party at the top chapel to mark the coronation of Her Majesty Queen Elizabeth II...

....While customers at the Farmyard also marked the occasion. They are, from the left: Ted Smith, Bill Shepherd, Johnnie Procter, Mrs Proctor, Derek Forrest, Mr Harrison (licensee), Dorothy Harrison, Brian Sheldon, Fred Billinge, Bernard Wragg, Tom Lievesley, Enos Wragg, Sid Gilbert, Freddie Birds.

There was obviously much celebration to mark the Jubilee of King George V in 1935:

The Boarding House Hotel in Alport was decorated.

A group of girls joining in the Jubilee celebrations. Among those who can be seen are Joyce Birds, Muriel Birds, Barbara Marsden, Drusilla Oldfield, Maud Shimwell and Doris Marshall.

The boys are in front of the bonfire built for the celebrations. They are: Back from the left: Eric Shimwell, Tom Craw, Bill Shimwell, Bob Rowland. Front: Tom Birds, John Brindley.

No celebration, ceremony or parade in Youlgrave would be complete without the Silver Band. It was founded over a hundred years ago at a time when many local villages had a band. The first set of instruments was purchased through the Cooperative Society shortly after it opened and the instruments were displayed in the window. According to a popular story, when the would-be bandsmen first took the instruments out in a procession, they sang 'pom, pom, pom' as they were unable to play. A pig looking over a wall is said to have joined in and this is supposed to be the origin of Youlgrave's local nickname 'Pommy'! Some of the original instruments are still in existence, although unplayable. More instruments were purchased after World War II following fund-raising events. Membership of the Band declined in the 1970s but with a great deal of dedication and the help of some newcomers

In 1992 John Roper conducts the band at the Blessing of the Wells.

it has kept going. Concerts sponsored by Derbyshire Dales District Council, and other events, help with income nowadays. There have been many conductors over the years, including Cornelius Roper, Herbert Shimwell, Mike Hargreaves, Billy Hawley, Raymond Brassington, Neville Riley, David Mason, Steve Sutton, Ann Underdown, Derek Holmes, Albert Shimwell, Jeremy Mold, John Roper and, at the time of writing, Graham Robinson.

In the early 1950s the band is seen marching past the Old Stables watched by Martin Fryer sitting on the gatepost.

A presentation to Cornelius Roper, John's grandfather, in 1957.

Cornelius Roper again. He conducted the band for many years until he retired at the age of 84 in 1957.

The band leaving the church at the Blessing of the Wells in 1979.

A very early band.

The band outside the Reading Room in the early part of the century. Some of the instruments can be clearly seen.

An early photo of the band in fine uniforms. Back row, from the right: Harry Evans, Frank Evans, Jimmy Slaney, Dickie Wain, ? , J H Purseglove; middle row, from the right: Albert Wragg, ? , Cornelius Roper, Charlie Wragg; front row, from the right: Will Sutton, Harry Evans.

The band in around 1900, believed to be at a contest at Hasland.

As well as the pantomime there is often other entertainment in the village. For a long period there was a very popular cinema at the Village Hall – the projection room can still be seen on the end of the building. There is a move afoot to start Youlgrave Cinema again in the near future. There is a long tradition of amateur dramatics, sadly in abeyance at the moment. We have had line-dancing, circle dancing and various other entertainments. Tea dances have become a popular fixture at the Village Hall. The pubs support quiz teams that regularly take part in local tournaments. As well as the Village Hall, other venues provide various entertainment. There are well-attended adult education classes at the newly refurbished Reading Room (built in 1857 and once the headquarters of the Youlgrave Literary Society). The Scout and Community Hut, rebuilt in the 1990s to replace the one that burned down in the early 1970s, is used for a variety of activities.

Though not strictly entertainment provided by and for the village, in 1969 there was great excitement when the film *The Virgin and the Gypsy* was filmed in and around Youlgrave. Many villagers were extras. At the village hall the 'Colgrave Players' performed a continental revue!

A press cutting of a concert at the Village Hall in 1960.

Raper Lodge was transformed into 'Colgrave' vicarage for the film and a garden built in front of the house. This photo was taken during the filming.

From the left: Sid Birds, Mildred and Helen Bacon dressed as extras for *The Virgin and the Gypsy*.

In 1986 a play depicting significant events in Youlgrave's history was performed in the church as part of celebrations marking the anniversary of the Domesday Book. A very large number of people were involved in writing, acting, and behind the scenes. In this photo the advent of the Waterworks is portrayed as a mummers' play. On the left is Peter Hill as the village doctor. Judith Green represents the Fountain. Andrew Bidmead wears a white-faced mask. Elizabeth Lomas is watching. Alan Brownlee is on the right.

Members of the cast in the history play. Back row, from the left: Russ Hubber, Bill Darley, Anne Billinge: front row from the left: Neil Ardley, Jane Ardley, Pat Cleaver, Mary Lievesley, Tessa Brough, Judith Green.

Paul Sansom (left) and Charlie Watson (right) enact the fight between Thomas Cokayne and Thomas Burdett which resulted in Cokayne's death in 1488 (See p.8 for Cokayne's tomb).

A bat-headed monster based on a carving in the church roof (see p.8) opened the play, performing a strange dance.

In a scene depicting events in the lives of the Cokayne and Shirley families in the 1400s, John McCaul serenades his wife Gloria who sits sewing.

In 1990 Youlgrave people had another chance to appear as extras, this time on the small screen. The well dressers were asked to prepare a dressing to be used in a commercial for a well-known mineral water. Villagers played the part of various rustics. In this photo, from the left are Abraham Twyford and Dougie Oldfield with another.

Another scene of rustic bliss for the commercial. Russ Hubber is standing holding the shepherd's crook and a lot of other people are having a very good time.

Frank Twyford and Dougie Oldfield.

The amateur players at the village hall have appeared under various names, among them the Village Hall Players, the Iola Players, and the Holywell Players. At the time of writing we have no regular group. In 1937, this performance of *Love from a Stranger* by Frank Vosper included Bernard Evans, Bernard Hadfield, Mr Birds, Mr Colman, Miss Hassill, Miss M Harrison, Miss E Oldfield and Mrs Lees.

We don't know what this play was. It was probably in the late 1920s, and we can only identify Bernard Hadfield on the extreme left, and Mrs. Lees on the right.

In the 1960s the cast of *Men in Shadows* included, from the left: Steve Walker, Harry Sandell, Jack Elliott, Susan Bourne, Norman Wilson, John Roper.

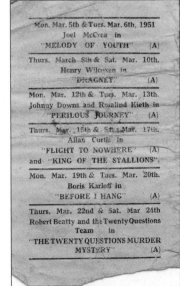

For many years the village hall was also the village cinema, providing entertainment several times a week. This is a programme from 1951 - it will probably cost rather more to get in when Youlgrave Cinema re-opens its doors.

Youlgrave now has three public houses: the George Hotel, the Bull's Head Hotel and the Farmyard. There was a fourth called the Thornhill Arms opposite the church and now the Dunn family home. Alport had the Boarding House Hotel which was demolished when the road was altered in 1937 (photographs of this appear in the chapters on Buildings and Transport). The pubs play an important part in village life providing meeting places for various societies and venues for social and sporting events. Pictures of them occur all through this book.

Prince Charles and John Brindley standing outside the George Hotel. In 1976 Prince Charles and Princess Alexandra attended the wedding of Elizabeth Waterhouse and Richard Beckett at All Saints' church. Prince Charles asked John Brindley if he and the Princess might "freshen up" at the George.

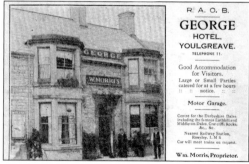

An advertising card for the George.

Mr & Mrs Clark (Peggy Bacon's parents) were licencees of the George from 1938 until the early 1950s. Peggy remembers initial difficulties in understanding the local accent. One comment: *"You munna say owt about nobody or you call the whole village"* refers to the fact that almost everybody was related to everybody else.

John Brindley and Sylvia Frost held their wedding reception at the Bull's Head in August 1947.

Waiting for Santa Claus to arrive outside the Bull's Head in 1988. Ann and Laura Knowles, Ian Wetherley and Mr Birds are among those present.

Mr Albert E Harrison behind the bar at the Farmyard. Mr Harrison was licensee for 40 years. His daughter Miss F K Harrison was granted the licence following his death in 1960. She and her sister Dorothy kept the pub until the late 1970s.

The Harrison family outside the Farmyard.

A trip made by Farmyard customers to a Cup Final in the 1920s.

Customers in the Farmyard. Bottom r. is Mighty Fine Rhodes in band uniform.

A lady with a bicycle - Mrs Brindley from the Bull's Head.

Annie Vera and Maud Greenhough on Conksbury Lane c.1900.

Margaret Folley and her father James, a mining engineer, in the late 1930s. The photograph was taken in Barnes Lane.

Thomas Birds at Old Hall Farm early in the twentieth century. He is with his daughter Sarah, who married Joseph Shimwell, and her daughter Polly. It is said that he used to take a bag of sovereigns on horseback to Liverpool to buy bulk corn and cattle, selling them on his way back.

Isobel Mosley (now Bailey) by the waterfall above the bridge at Alport with her toy yacht in 1949.

Season's Greetings

BETTY AND BERNARD WISH YOU ALL A MERRY OLD FASHIONED CHRISTMAS WITH PEACE & GOOD HEALTH IN 1998

Bernard and Betty Oldfield, splendid in Victorian costume, during his leadership of the Derbyshire Dales District Council.

Village Hall worthies: Jim Evans, Mick Roper and Don Bateman.

A family group from the 1920s showing Lillian Buxton (née Thompson), Annette Oldfield's grandmother, with David, Mary, Samuel and the baby Elizabeth. She was widowed in her thirties when her husband Samuel Buxton died from wounds sustained in World War I.

Lillian Clark (née Oldfield) long before she became Chairman of the Parish Council.

The wedding in the 1930s of Amy Evans and Ben Gladwin who are in the centre. On the left Jack Wragg is standing next to the bridesmaid Doris Evans. On the right Ben Evans stands next to the other bridesmaid Mary Evans. The child is Elizabeth ?. They are outside Braemar House on Main Street.

Roger Bacon (longtime Chairman of the Waterworks) smoking a clay pipe at the last Barmote Court he attended at the Moot Hall in Wirksworth (he died in 1996). He represented the *liberty* of Youlgrave.

Martha Prime, now in her eighties, spends much of her time knitting for various charities. She has received several awards in recognition of her work. This award was part of the Chairman's Community Award Scheme.

Norman Wilson was Chairman of Derbyshire County Council 1967-1969 and 1977-1981. He inaugurated the Civic Service and is seen greeting guests at the first service at All Saints' Church in 1968. He was also Chairman of the Peak Park Planning Board 1981-1985.

Enjoying a ride on a farm cart in 1951 are, from l: Lucy Wardle, Dorothy Sandell, Harry Sandell behind Marjorie and Gillian Wardle.

Martha Shimwell, wife of James Shimwell, in c. 1900.

James Fryer with his grandfather James Shimwell outside Old Hall Farm in c. 1928.

The Walker family in Alport. Back row from l: Claud Elliott, Matt Wright, Tom Walker, Noel Walker, Anthony Walker, Tom Shimwell. In the middle: Cathy Twyford. Front row, from l: Mary Walker, Mary Elliott, Mrs Walker, Patty Wright, Alice Shimwell.

Harry Holland in about 1923.

Thomas Wardle at Church Farm in the 1960s.

Mr Coates, who lived at the cottages now called Tweedledee and Tweedledum, was grandfather of Maggie Coates who used to work at Beryl Buxton's shop. He had a smallholding and also swept roads to supplement his income. He is pictured in Alport sometime between the two World Wars.

Charlie Wardle in 1913.

Someone, in August 1919, wrote those words on a postcard. He, or she, was quite right.

However, it was not always quite so peaceful as the picture of Conksbury Bridge suggests. The photograph (p.76) in the industry section is a reminder of mining in Lathkill Dale. Since Roman times the White Peak has been mined for lead and for centuries the whole area echoed to the sounds of miners at work. Lead was smelted in Alport, bobbins were made in Middleton Dale, waterwheels turned.

Nowadays some workings are reopened for the extraction of fluorspar but essentially what was once an industrial area is now a haven for wild flowers and wildlife. To live here is a privilege which it is easy to take for granted until reminded of it by the sight of a young dipper in Bradford Dale or the view down Moor Lane. The beautiful stone walls are one of the delights of the White Peak. One limestone quarry was near here and the gritstone can be seen across the valley, so Youlgrave houses can have a dramatic mixture of limestone and gritstone.

In 1902 the Rev. W Parker Stamper's book on the village included details of accommodation. Mrs J H Salt in Church Street, Miss Marion Thompson near the church, Mrs John Shimwell in Alport Lane and others offered apartments, some offered a piano. The George and the Bull's Head mention cyclists particularly.

The Reverend is sometimes carried away by his enthusiasm—' Dear, lovely old Youlgrave, ...The heart of man rejoices as he views the immovable in nature, the everlasting hills, the valleys still so still and peaceful, trodden in past days by foot of warrior, priest and peasant, trodden today by those who love their native land and home, and find in it the same old fixed and settled line of work and duty, as in former days their ancestors were wont to pursue.' Though his style is more flowery than we expect nowadays, we can appreciate his sentiments.

Mrs Josie Wright remembers nostalgically the Back Lane from Conksbury, early in the twentieth century, grassed over and bordered with hawthorn and wild flowers.

At the end of the nineteenth and the beginning of the twentieth century the cultivated north side of Bradford Dale was much admired and compared by one visitor to the terraced fields of Valparaiso in South America, so that it came to be known as Valpo. Later it reverted to nature but now an attempt is being made to re-establish it.

In 1928 the French painter Lucien Pissarro stayed with Miss Hayes at Coldwell End and Ivor Hayes carried his easel. She was 'nice and obliging and everything is clean'. He was not so happy with the village women with 'dirty, bawling youngsters' gossiping just where he wanted to paint.

Raenstor Rock enticed climbers at a time when the Peak District was becoming a major rock-climbing area.

In recent years winters have been mild, but in past years the seasons have been more clearly defined, with some dramatic, snowy winters. None was quite so dramatic as the great snow of 1614, described graphically in the Accounts of the Churchwardens of that date—'This year 1614 Jan 16 began the greatest snow that ever fell within mans memory. It covered the earth five quarters deep upon the plain. And for heaps or drifts of snow they were very deep; so that passengers both horse and foot, passed over gates and hedges and walls—it continued until the 12th day of March without the sight of any earth.'

Friden in 1947.

Raper Bridge in 1979.

By comparison the gentle picture above suggests a light breeze and soft light. This is Alport at its most delightful, with walkers going towards the old mill and waterwheel happily ignoring the No Entry sign. A corn mill at Alport was mentioned in Domesday Book. It was rolling oats up to the 1950s, then became a corn store and a trout hatchery, a long and active history.

The pleasures of water, to look at or be in. Above Alport Bridge, below the bottom of Bradford after heavy rain.

Alport in the 1930s.

Bankside at its most lush, looking up from the Fisherman's Cottage in the 1950s, with Herbert Wright in a doorway, holding a newspaper.